Finland As It Is - Primary Source Edition

Harry De Windt

FINLAND AS IT IS

BY HARRY DE WINDT, F.R.G.S.

AUTHOR OF "THE NEW SIBERIA," "A RIDE TO INDIA," "THROUGH ALASKA TO
BÉRING STRAITS," "TRUE TALES OF TRAVEL," ETC., ETC.

WITH ILLUSTRATIONS

NEW YORK
E. P. DUTTON AND COMPANY
1910

PRINTED IN GREAT BRITAIN

TO

HYLDA DE WINDT

PREFACE

THIS record of a very pleasurable journey was only published at the suggestion, in St. Petersburg, of an English bookseller. "During the summer season," said the latter, "I am pestered every day for books upon Finland. But what am I to do? There are none in the market. Most people have read Mrs. Tweedie's *Through Finland*, everybody carries a 'Murray's Guide,' but there is nothing new on the subject. Why don't you write your experiences? Tell people in England and America how to get to Finland, and how to travel through it as pleasantly and as cheaply as possible, and I will answer for the sale of the book—at any rate in Petersburg."

Thus this little volume, compiled from very crude and careless notes, has seen the light. I have entered into minute details regarding hotels, trains, steamers, shops, etc., for the convenience of travellers (who will also find a short glossary of Finnish words), and may add that the great charm of Finland lies in the fact that one may explore its wildest districts in comfort, if not in absolute luxury. The following trip, for instance, can easily be accomplished by the most delicate invalid of either sex, with the exception, perhaps, of the drive from Uleåborg to the head of the Gulf of Bothnia; and even this short land journey may be avoided by taking the sea route from Uleåborg direct to Luleå, whence there is direct and frequent communication by rail with Stockholm and the rest of Europe.

I take this opportunity of thanking my many friends in Finland for their valuable assistance in the compilation of this work, and I should add that a great deal of the information anent the geography, etc., of the country, contained in the twelfth chapter, was obtained from Mr. O. M. Reuter's *Finlande et Les Finlandais*, published at Helsingfors in 1889.

HARRY DE WINDT

45, Avenue Kleber
Paris
August, 1901

CONTENTS

LIST OF ILLUSTRATIONS

FULL PAGE

IN THE TEXT

FINLAND AS IT IS

CHAPTER I

SAINT PETERSBURG

"AND this is Saint Petersburg!"

The speaker turns from the window with a yawn of disgust, sinks into an armchair, and resumes his perusal of the *Times* (five days old) in despair. He is an English tourist who, with a party of equally deluded mortals, has come here expecting to find the place a vortex of life and gaiety. I often wonder why the dullest capital in Europe is generally so depicted by the British novelist. Moscow is a dream of beauty; Odessa, a little Paris; but for dulness, damp, and discomfort commend me to the city of gloom on the banks of the Neva. The buildings are tawdry, the streets ill-paved, and a general air of stagnation pervades even the

B

busiest quarters.   The most fashionable hotel is,
according to modern ideas, a very second-rate
establishment, and save the " Opera," there is
not a theatre worthy of the name in the place.
The Winter Palace, one or two churches, and
the Hermitage are certainly worth seeing, for
the collection of paintings by the old masters in
the latter is probably unique.   But with these
two exceptions there is scarcely an object of
interest save the fortress of SS. Peter and Paul,
which, by the way, may now be visited throughout, as political prisoners are no longer immured
in its dark dungeons below the level of the Neva.
The fortress of Schlüsselburg, on Lake Ladoga,
has taken its place as a place of detention, which
is far more dreaded (if English people only knew
it) than much-maligned Siberia.

As to the climate!   Well, Saint Petersburg is
built upon a swamp.   To-day, although the sun
is shining brightly at Kronstadt, here we are
choking in dense fog, and a drizzly rain is falling.
It is but five o'clock on a July afternoon, but
lamps are lit, not the bright electric lights of
civilisation, but dull gas-jets that only serve to
heighten the depressing aspect of this gloomy
reading-room with its bare walls and comfortless
furniture.   One of the saddest sights I ever saw

was in this very apartment: a young Frenchman who, carried away by the Parisian enthusiasm over the Franco-Russian alliance, had come to Petersburg expecting to find a second Lutetia. But his stay was limited to forty-eight hours and he spent most of that time in this gloomy room immersed in the antediluvian volumes of *Punch*, which form the sole literary solace of unhappy guests. And yet this is the best hotel in the place, and its charges almost equal those of the " Ritz " establishments.

We read (in English novels) of clear sunshine, and dainty sleighs sliding swiftly over the snow to the music of silver bells. We picture stately palaces, glittering restaurants, furs, diamonds, and a general atmosphere of dazzling splendour. This is all a myth. Wealth and luxury no doubt exist, and in the highest degree, but only in a select circle as unapproachable, by most foreigners, as the North Pole itself. For the average tourist, Petersburg means boredom throughout the twenty-four hours. During summer the islands are amusing enough in the evening, but in winter the theatres are depressingly dull, unless a star of the Sara Bernhardt type happens to be acting, and even then the discomfort of a draughty or overheated house renders the artistic treat a questionable pleasure. All the music-halls are beneath contempt, and should be entered with caution and a supply of Keating's powder. On the other hand, there is no early-closing movement, and you can eat your supper in comfort, and remain if so disposed until the small hours at the principal restaurants. The Russians are great supper-eaters. They will think nothing of following up a hearty meal at midnight, say at Cubat's famous house, with another towards dawn at Filipof's, or the Mali Yaroslav. But a Russian digestion is needed to accomplish this gastronomic feat, especially as such items as rump-steak, stewed venison, and even roast sucking-pig generally figure on the menu.

As for the Nevsky Prospekt, it is, even in the height of the season, a dreary, colourless thoroughfare, far less attractive than Piccadilly. For the former is abominably paved, generally ankle deep in mud and slush, while tawdry American street cars and shabby "droshkies" replace the brilliant equipages which only exist in the fertile brain of the London journalist. Even the finest shops present a poor appearance, with their tawdry sign-boards, illustrating, in the crudest style and colour, the nature of their wares. The promiscuous manner, too, in which the wealthiest and poorest business houses are jumbled together is as unique as it is confusing to a stranger. You may see a plate-glass window blazing with priceless gems, and next to it a dark, dirty little shop for the sale of old clothes ; while in another street a purveyor of salt fish and cheap groceries will be dispensing his unsavoury wares under the nose of a fashionable florist. No wonder that the Russian capital has a cheerless, squalid look even in the sunshine, which is seldom seen between autumn and springtime, when the fogs that rise from the Neva are even denser than those of the Thames ! I have lived here during every season of the year. In May, when the ice-bound canals break up, poisoning the air with the stench of sewage ; in July, when the heat and dust are unbearable. In winter all who can do so seek sunshine on the Riviera. Early autumn is perhaps the most favourable season for those visiting Petersburg on business. No sane being would willingly do so at any time for pleasure.

My business had, upon this occasion, been unsuccessful. It was on the 25th of July, 1900, that I set out from Paris for New York by land (on behalf of the *Daily Express* of London),

C

viâ Siberia, Bering Straits, and Alaska. A portion of this journey (as far as the Chinese frontier) would have to be accomplished by the Trans-Siberian Railway. But the outbreak of hostilities in the far East was destined to upset all my plans, as an interview with the Secretary for Foreign Affairs plainly showed. " I regret to say that you cannot travel by the Trans - Siberian Railway," said Count L. conclusively, " at any rate, for the present. The line is now under the sole control of the military authorities, and only a limited number of our own Press correspondents may use it." Thus the long voyage of exploration upon which I had lavished months of careful preparation was for a time at least knocked upon the head, for experience has shown me that, in matters of this kind, the Russian statesman is adamant. And the success of the undertaking depended so much upon the punctuality of my arrival at Nijni-Kolymsk (a remote settlement on the Arctic Ocean) that a wild idea of posting the whole distance was at once abandoned. So I returned disconsolately home, resolved to return by the night mail to Paris.

But fate had other plans in store. I was partaking of " zakouski," that invariable pre-

liminary to meals in Russia, at my hotel, when
a stranger with whom I had travelled from
Berlin approached the "buffet," and while dally-
ing with fresh caviare and other dainties expressed
regret at the failure of my overland voyage, in
which he had displayed some interest. He was
middle-aged, with a flaxen beard and clear blue
eyes, and was attired in garments of shiny broad-
cloth, which, at first sight, suggested commercial
travel or the mercantile marine. The man's
nationality was a puzzle, for he spoke English
without a trace of foreign accent, and French
and German with almost equal facility. At first
I put him down as a Pole, for his hatred of
Russia was aired with a recklessness that
occasionally caused me some anxiety. To-night
the mystery was solved. "You have time on
your hands," said my mysterious friend, as we
sat down to dinner. "Why not visit my country?
What is it?" he laughingly added, adjusting his
napkin previous to an attack on a savoury plate
of "bortsch." "Ah! to be sure, I have not told
you. Why, Finland!"

Finland! The name was of course familiar,
but was suggestive chiefly of pine forests, tar,
and timber, with a squalid fishing village thrown
in here and there; a wild, barren province,

quite a century behind the times, and likely
to remain so. My knowledge of the people
was equally vague. The only Finn I had
hitherto met was a harpooner on an American
whaler, a surly, occasionally inebriated individual,
who inspired me with anything but respect for
his country or compatriots. But Mr. D.'s glow-
ing accounts of Finland, her wonderful cities and
boundless resources, fairly took my breath away,
and I rose from the table half inclined to travel
homewards through this remarkable land which
even educated Englishmen regard as a primitive
state, but little in advance of its northern neighbour, Lapland. I must own that, until D. enlightened my ignorance, I had always done so
and although disposed at first to discredit the
dazzling picture drawn by my friend of his native
land, I subsequently found that it was by no
means exaggerated.

A discussion which lasted far into the night
ended in my resolve to start on the morrow for
Viborg, the frontier town of the Grand Duchy.
"You will then go to Helsingfors," said D.,
tracing my journey through the country upon the
map, and ending with a flourish of the forefinger
on an apparently obscure settlement at the head
of the Gulf of Bothnia. " But it will take

months!" I argued, with a lively recollection of my snail-like progress over the post-roads of Russian Asia. "Days, if you wish it," quietly rejoined D., adding contemptuously, "Finland is not Siberia. You need never leave the railway until you reach Uleåborg. Thence you will drive or go by steamer to Luleå, on the Swedish coast (three or four days by land), and from Luleå the railway will take you on to Stockholm. A charming trip. How long? It can be done in a fortnight, but I predict that, once in Finland, you will be in no hurry to leave it!"

And he was right.

CHAPTER II

VIBORG

RAILWAY travelling in Russia, if somewhat slow according to modern ideas, is infinitely more comfortable than in other parts of Europe. The corridor cars are roomy and cunningly contrived so as to afford warmth or coolness at will. The station restaurants are generally excellent, the prices moderate, meals well served, and a reasonable time allowed for their consumption. You are not expected to make a repast off flyblown buns and leathery sandwiches, as in England, or to bolt a dinner of five courses in as many minutes, as in France. The traveller will find a good cuisine and wines, bright silver, glass, and flowers, even on the remote railway across the Oural Mountains. Indeed, I am told that the Trans-Siberian line provides pianos, libraries, and even bathrooms for its guests.

But to return to more civilised regions. The

well-known "Compagnie des Wagon Lits" is in
operation over most of the lines in European
Russia, but the Finland State Railway (by
which I was about to travel) provides its own
sleeping accommodation. This consists of two
berthed compartments, which may be retained by
one person at a trifling cost. Indeed, the railway
fares throughout Finland are absurdly low as
compared with those of other countries. You
may obtain a circular ticket over the whole
Finnish railway system for about thirty shillings,
and thus travel seventeen hundred miles for the
price of a return ticket between London and
Hastings!

When D. accompanied me on the following
evening to the railway station, we found the
platforms crowded with a regiment of Cossacks
bound for Helsingfors. A number of officers
had assembled to bid their comrades farewell,
and the sound of laughter and the popping of
champagne corks issuing from a brightly lit
saloon carriage especially aroused the ire of my
companion, whose scathing remarks as to Russian officers in general and these in particular
were fortunately not overheard. My Finnish
friend was, of course, biassed, and therefore
unjust. I have met with Russian regiments in

all parts of the Empire, have roughed it with
Siberian Cossacks on ice-bound Sakhalin, and
dined in civilisation with the Chevaliers
Gardes, and have invariably found their officers
as courteous and well bred as those of other
countries. Most English travellers can testify
to their hospitality, and even D. could not accuse
them of want of pluck. On the other hand,
the Russian Tommy Atkins is anything but a
showy personage. His shabby white cap, drab
overcoat (often patched and darned), and rusty
high-boots present a sorry spectacle after the
bright, showy uniforms of Vienna and Berlin;
and yet, notwithstanding clumsy, ill-fitting garments, there is a dogged, workmanlike look
about the troops of the Tsar that inspires confidence, while their arms and accoutrements
sparkle like silver. "Fritz" may look very
pretty on parade, but give me "Ivan" on active
service—especially on short rations and poor pay.

Bidding adieu to D., who kindly provided me
with several letters of introduction, I entered the
train, and by eleven o'clock the lights of Petersburg were dim on the horizon. To my surprise a
severe-looking elderly lady shortly afterwards
appeared with sheets and pillows, for only female
attendants are employed on Finnish sleeping-

cars. My destination, Viborg, was to be reached
at 2 a.m., and I therefore explained, in Russian,
that I should not need my bed, but the reply was
a blank stare. I had yet to learn that, as a rule,
the Finnish and Swedish languages only are

"A SEVERE-LOOKING ELDERLY LADY"

spoken in Finland, occasionally German or
French, but Russian never, if it can possibly be
avoided. My directions in French were at once
obeyed by the matron in question, who, although
probably conversant with Russian, flatly refused

to speak it. Finnish completely differs from all other European languages, and is even more complicated and difficult to acquire than Russian. It has a soft, musical sound, well adapted for music and poetry, while its extensive vocabulary consists of over 200,000 words. At one time the Russian tongue was almost compulsory, but this law has been gradually modified until, at the present day, it is only taught as a matter of form in the schools and universities.

There are few countries so absolutely dissimilar (save climatically) as Russia proper and Finland. Everything is different, commencing with the currency, for roubles and kopeks have now disappeared to give place to pennis and marks, the latter being equal to a French franc.* The contrast is especially noticeable as regards towns and their inhabitants. Thus there are few cities in European Russia which do not appear dreary and depressing to a stranger. Moscow and Odessa are exceptions, for the first named is undoubtedly picturesque, while the gardens, boulevards, and well-paved thoroughfares of the other present a striking contrast to, say, Kharkoff, with its general impression of gloom, and even squalor. Viborg is barely

* 100 pennis go to a mark.

eighty miles from Petersburg, and yet I awaken to-day in another world in a cosy bedroom worthy of the Gordon Hotels. Its windows overlook a scene more suggestive of sunny Spain or Italy than the Frozen North. The picturesque town nestling against a background of pine forest, and blue waters of the harbour sparkling under a cloudless sky, the wooded islets with their pretty villas, the ruined castle of Viborg, with its crumbling thirteenth-century battlements, and . last, but not least, the general air of life and animation are indeed pleasant to contemplate after the drab, dreary streets of the Russian capital. Viborg is, perhaps, the least imposing of all Finnish towns, for many of its dwellings are built of wood, which, however, is generally stained a dark red colour, cleaner and more cheerful-looking than rough, weather-bleached logs. Pleasant also is it to saunter through the picturesque old streets, to ransack the silver shops, and come suddenly upon a market-place, lying in the shadow of quaint old gabled houses, where the rosy-cheeked peasants, carts and cobbles, and canvas booths packed with fruit and vegetables recall some old-world town in far-away Brittany. Everything has a cleanly, bright appearance, and the fresh, pine-scented sea-breeze is grateful indeed after muggy, in-odorous Petersburg.

There is time before breakfast for a look at the famous old castle, which stands on an adjacent island. I am ferried to it by an ancient Finn, who speaks English, and who is full of whaling experiences and an enthusiastic admira-tion for South Shields as a mercantile and social centre. My guide points out various shot marks on the massive walls, for this brave old ruin has weathered many a fierce battle since its erection by the Swedish patriot, Torkel Knutson, in 1293. On relanding I present my old friend with the Finnish equivalent for a threepenny-bit, and although the trip has occupied nearly an hour, he is delighted. Then back to the hotel through the public gardens, now crowded with fashionably dressed loungers, for Viborg, although it contains but some 20,000 inhabitants, is the Brighton of Northern Russia. At the inn I find that an excellent repast has been specially prepared by mine host for his two English guests, for in Finland nothing is too good for the "Englantiläinen."*

As he himself would probably have put it, the other Englishman is an Irishman, a cheery, amus-

* Englishman.

ing fellow from County Wicklow, with whom I am presently seated at a snowy table overlooking the harbour, dotted with the white sails of pleasure yachts. The menu is preceded by the invariable "smörgasbord," which is partaken of standing at the bar of the restaurant. "Smörgasbord" begins with a nip of cognac, or something else,

A RUSSIAN BRIGHTON

from a large silver vessel with a tap for each liqueur. This receptacle is called the "branvinn," and towers over a score or more of small glass dishes, containing dainty appetisers, such as salmon, smoked and raw, caviare, pink and grey (the former delicious); all kinds of fish, fresh, salted, and in aspic jelly; smoked reindeer and potted meats of all kinds. A preliminary meal of

D

this kind is, perhaps, more calculated to appease than to whet a British appetite, but we were still able to do justice to some delicious crayfish and roast partridges, washed down by a bottle of Crimean claret. Viborg is famous for its crayfish, and the French " écrevisse," excellent though it be, is not to be compared with this northern delicacy, although the latter are sold for something like a shilling a hundred in the markets of Åbo and Helsingfors. It would almost pay to export a few thousands every year to Paris, where such outrageous prices are charged for that exquisite creation, " Soupe à la Bisque." Coffee and liqueurs are served in the garden below, and so pleasant and enlivening has been the meal, that by the time cigars are alight I feel equal to any emergency, even to accompanying my Irish friend to Imatrá, that fisherman's paradise, for which he has this season forsaken the lakes and rivers of the Emerald Isle.

But mine host will not hear of our departure—at any rate, until the morrow—for he has been deputed to invite us to a party which is to take place that evening at the villa of a friend on a neighbouring lake. There will be dancing and fireworks and other attractions of a festive nature

on the occasion of the marriage of a daughter of
the house.   Besides, the one steamer of the day
for Imatrá has already left Viborg, which clinches
the matter.   The son of Erin accepts with some
reluctance, for dancing and dress are less in his

A SON OF ERIN

line than flies and fishing-rods, and his wardrobe
consists wholly of hobnails and homespun.   I am
not sorry, however, to seize this opportunity of
seeing the well-to-do Finn at home, especially
under such agreeable circumstances.

A ball in Finland is a serious business, not to

be lightly undertaken. On this occasion the scene of the revels was comparatively near, about twenty miles away, but guests often travel double the distance to a dance, and leave home at mid-day gaily attired in evening dress, only to return to their beds twenty-four hours later. When we embarked, towards 5 p.m., on the little steamer chartered for the occasion, we found her decks crowded with ladies in ball-gowns, and most of the men in the orthodox white tie and swallow-tail, although one unconventional youth had adopted light grey trousers and a cerulean scarf. But everyone on board, old and young, were gay, good-humoured, and scrupulously polite, for there is no country in Europe where a stranger of any nationality meets with such cordial hospitality as in Finland.

The villa of our host was situated on a beautiful lake, a veritable inland sea, surrounded by low, pine-clad hills. For some distance we skirted the shore with its garden - girt villas dotted promiscuously about, as though, like stones, they had been cast haphazard by some giant hand into the dark green forest. One of these rustic dwellings cost a fabulous sum, a portion of its grounds being laid out to repre-sent a miniature tract of Finnish scenery. The

Finns, like the French, know how to make the most of picturesque nature, for although Russia is, in parts, almost as beautiful as its Grand Duchy, the loveliest spots are generally marred by neglect and untidiness. In and around the towns of Finland every scrap of greenery is tended as carefully as though this were a desert instead of a well-wooded land, while in summer-time the humblest peasant takes care to surround his abode with wild but fragrant shrubs and flowers.

The bride and bridegroom had departed when we arrived at dusk, to find Mr. Lindström's villa ablaze with light. Adjoining it was a separate building of wood, with a floor of polished "parquet," which had been specially constructed for a ballroom. The latter is a common adjunct to Finnish country houses, for here all classes (and all ages) are passionately fond of dancing. Even the tiniest village has its weekly dance on Saturday evenings in the largest available cottage or farm. The Lindströms' ballroom could have accommodated a couple of hundred guests, although we numbered under fifty. The room was gaily decorated with flags, ferns, and flowers, with a huge block

E

of lake-ice at each end of the apartment, which
contained no seats of any kind. For there were
no wallflowers, the most venerable couples
circling gravely round to the strains of an excellent string band, which, to my surprise, dis-
coursed the very latest dance music. I was
prepared in these remote regions to hear the
valses and polkas of my childhood, but the ball
was opened by a tuneful measure from the
" Belle of New York !"

The Villa Aura was, inside and out, a marvel
of symmetry and good taste. A stretch of smooth
sward sloped downwards from the house to the
lake, about a quarter of a mile from the building,
a two-storied one built in bungalow style, with
verandahs and French windows opening on the
lawn. The drawing-room was a spacious apartment, where shaded lamps threw a cool, dim
light over a quiet and cosy interior, to which
Algerian and Turkish rugs and lounges and a
Cairene " mashrabia " lent an oriental look. On
the walls were oil paintings by well-known
French and English artists, and a mezzotint of
Bartolozzi stood on an easel by the grand
piano. Looking around me at spreading
ferns, bowls of cut flowers, silver nicknacks,
and French novels that littered the tables, I

could scarcely realise that this was *my* Finland of a week ago. Mr. Lindström was a man of literary as well as artistic tastes, and I could willingly have passed hours in his library replete with rare and valuable books of all ages and languages. My host was justly proud of his unique collection of Finnish authors, but a modern production, in the shape of an atlas of Finland, published at Helsingfors, excited my especial admiration. For in the thirty odd maps it contains the population, meteorology, schools, agriculture, mines, forests, industries, communications, telegraphs, and even lighthouses are described and classified with a care and detail that must have entailed years of labour and research.* I doubt if any other country in the world can boast of such a complete geographical and statistical volume of reference, and therefore expressed surprise that so valuable a contribution to geographical literature was not more widely disseminated. "Because, my dear sir," replied Lindström warmly, "Finland is not yet known. Pray accept the atlas, and take it to England, where the majority of people seem to think that we live for nothing else in the world but tar and timber!" I

---

* *Atlas de Finlande*. Helsingfors, 1899. Société Anonyme. F. TILGMANN.

thanked my host for his valuable gift, but did not add that a very brief knowledge of his country had enlightened at least one British ignoramus!

A jolly-looking professor from the Helsingfors University, and one of his colleagues, a vacant-looking individual in spectacles, who resembled an elderly Verdant Green, joined us during this colloquy. "Our map shows our politics, sir," said the former, removing a huge china pipe which seldom left his lips. "You see," added the old man, shaking with laughter and pointing to a map of Finland, "she snaps her fingers at Sweden and kicks Russia in the eye!" And the coincidence of the configuration is indeed remarkable, as the reader will find on consulting an atlas. Verdant Green was then entering into further details, but as he did so Lindström and the professor quietly vanished from the library. They evidently knew their friend's proclivities. I have come across bores in all parts of the world, but this was indeed the cruellest and most persistent one that it has ever been my misfortune to encounter. Happily a cheery major, all gold lace and whiskers, soon came to the rescue, and carried me off to supper at midnight, but it was three o'clock in the morning before the last mazurka wound up the proceedings. To dance the Russian mazurka is an art in which few excel. But a younger sister of the bride moved through the quaint, gavotte-like measure with the grace and charm of an Otero. This northern dance has as many figures as a cotillon, and sometimes lasts for an hour or more.

And so, the last farewells exchanged, we re-embarked on the little steamer which was to bear us homewards. Most of the fair sex retired below to snatch a hurried rest, for the homes of many lay far beyond Viborg, but we remained on deck to enjoy the glorious scenery and fresh night air. Never shall I forget the exquisite beauty of that still, placid lake, studded with the reflection of a myriad stars, the coloured sidelights of passing steamers that flitted like glowworms over its surface, and the low, dark shores where the dull yellow glimmer of a cottage casement here and there showed that early risers were already astir. Once the vessel was made fast to land a few of our companions, and they grouped together on the little jetty as we glided away, and serenaded us. I can remember the air now, a part-song in minor, which sounded inexpressibly sweet and mournful as it died away in the dark, silent pine forest. The trip was like a scene from fairyland, which only ended as we neared the towering citadel, white houses, and shipping of Viborg, now wreathed in the grey mists of dawn.

CHAPTER III

IMATRÁ

THERE are three ways of reaching Imatrá from Viborg: (1) By rail and diligence; (2) by steamer and diligence; and (3) by the postroad. The first and last are not to be recommended, for the railway journey is uninteresting, and entails a tiresome change at the Simola Junction. In this case the traveller leaves the train at Villmanstrand, and drives the remainder of the distance along a fine bit of road skirting Lake Saima to Imatrá. Posting the whole distance is rough and tedious work, which can easily be avoided by embarking (as we did) on a comfortable steamer, equal in every respect to those of the Rhine or Danube, and proceeding *viâ* the Saima Canal as far as Rattijarvi. Here you will find a well-appointed diligence to convey you the remainder of the trip (about twenty-three English miles) to the falls. By this route the entire journey from Viborg to Imatrá occupies about seven hours, and costs (first class) eleven marks.

I was not returning to Viborg, and therefore left it with all my impedimenta, consisting of a couple of large, *cornerless* leather bags* (with stout locks), a frieze ulster, and a kodak. I mention the first-named, as they are indispensable on journeys where posting may occur in the itinerary. A long experience of this kind of travel in Siberia and other remote countries has convinced me that these bags are the best, for they have no sharp corners to disturb the traveller's rest or reveries over rough, stony roads. Moreover, their capacity is limitless, and I easily stowed away a fur coat (indispensable here in the early autumn) in addition to a liberal allowance of clothes, boots, books, and, when necessary, provisions. On this trip a heavy, hard portmanteau would prove an endless source of trouble and discomfort. I enter into these details for the benefit of those who, unacquainted with the peculiarities of Finnish travel, may follow in my footsteps.

We find many overnight acquaintances already assembled on the steamer which is bearing them homewards. Some have evidently not been to

* To be obtained of Silver and Co., Cornhill, E.C.

bed, for a sprinkling of the younger men are still in evening dress. A sable swallow-tail in broad daylight is generally suggestive of dissipation, not to say excess, but although our friends are gaily discussing the dance with many a merry jest and peal of laughter, there is not the faintest sign to show that any of the male sex have taken more wine than is good for them. Everyone is on deck enjoying the bright sunshine and crisp, bracing air. Here is our good friend the Herr Professor, who removes, for an instant only, the eternal china bowl to wish us good day, and beckons a pretty daughter to his side. Mademoiselle, notwithstanding fatigue and excitement, looks as fresh as a daisy, and greets us with a pleasant smile. She is now clad in a neat, tailor-made gown (for which I find Redfern is responsible), and looks as if she had just stepped out of the Rue de la Paix. Here, too, is the Herr Major, who has discarded his full-dress war-paint for a cool linen tunic with gold shoulder-straps, and looks all the better for it, while behind him (oh, horror!) loom the gleaming gig-lamps of the Bore, who instantly buttonholes me anent the foreign policy of England. I elude him by joining a joyous band of students in a glass of champagne below, but the Bore follows like a shadow, and while sipping his wine, confidentially invites me to explain the Irish question. This is too much, and I pass him on to the man from Wicklow,

"THE BORE"

who silently writhes in his grasp, while I make my escape.

> " I do not tremble when I meet
>   The stoutest of my foes;
> But Heaven defend me from the man
>   Who never, never goes !"

The profusion and inanity of Verdant Green's

questions recalled a famous *mot* of poor Andrée's, when driven to distraction by a talkative neighbour at a dinner party, just before his last voyage. "But how will you know when you have really crossed the North Pole, Professor?" was the question, preceded by many other equally silly remarks. "Oh, that will be simple enough, Madame," replied Andrée, with his well-known dry humour; "a north wind will become a south one!"

The Saima Canal was completed in 1856, at a cost of about half a million sterling. It is under forty miles in length, is navigable for vessels drawing eight feet, and unites Lake Ladoga with the Gulf of Bothnia *viâ* the "Lake of a Thousand Isles," or Lake Saima. The fall from the latter to the coast necessitated the construction of no less than twenty-eight locks, splendidly built of the granite of the country. Finland is famous for its granite, and has furnished the material for many of the monuments, quays, and bridges in Petersburg. Porphyry is also found in the island of Hogland, and the slab over the tomb of Napoleon I. at the "Invalides," in Paris, was brought thence.

From an engineering point of view the Saima Canal is a masterpiece, and the country through

which it passes is justly regarded as one of the
beauty-spots of Finland. Our little ship glides
smoothly at first past belts of dark pine forest—
cool, fragrant, and as silent as the grave—through
which the narrow waterway winds like a thread
of silver, to debouch at intervals, with a warm
gush of sunshine, into the open country. Here
are green meadows and rippling brooks, with
lazy cattle browsing knee-deep in the rich grass,
and ferns and wild flowers fringing the water's
edge. A small lake is crossed, and we arrive at
Juustila, a favourite summer resort of the people
of Viborg, with an hotel and some pretty private
dwellings. We re-enter the canal, and now
comes a siding—for only one vessel can pass
abreast—and we tie up for a while and saunter
through some peaceful village with white villas
rising here and there amongst the dark wooden
dwellings of the poor. The former are surrounded by trim gardens, where "Gloire de
Dijon" roses, heliotrope, and jasmine bloom in
sweet profusion; and there are creepers, striped
sunblinds, and tennis lawns, just as though a bit
of the Thames around Cookham or Sunbury had
dropped out of the blue northern sky. Then
back to our boat, laden with baskets full of
"mjod," clotted cream, and berries which are

sold at every lock by blue-eyed, flaxen-haired children. We are too late for the wild strawberry (the "mansikker"), which is so common in June and July that this country is known as "Strawberry Land" as well as "The Land of a Thousand Lakes." But there are many other wild berries not to be despised ; for instance, the "Vatuka," or wild raspberry, the "Puolukka," or cranberry, and especially the "Suomurain," a kind of yellow raspberry now at its best. "Mjod" is a local product—a kind of effervescing cider— which, when iced, forms a refreshing and harmless summer drink.

By one o'clock we are at Rattijarvi, at the northern extremity of the lake of that name. It is a pretty spot with an excellent hotel, where we are invited to share the dainty luncheon thoughtfully ordered beforehand by the Professor. My neighbour at table is the Herr Major, who is returning to Villmanstrand, where his regiment is brigaded, with several others, under canvas. I mention that having asked my way of a soldier, in the Russian language, in the streets of Viborg, my inquiry met with no response. "There is nothing strange about that," says the Major. "We have no Russians in our army." The uniform is, however, precisely similar, except that

F

in Finland blue, instead of red, facings are worn.
The white, linen, soup-platelike caps are the same
in summer; and in winter the astrakhan head-
dress is identical; in fact, outwardly, the Finnish
officer exactly resembles his Russian brother-in-

" HERR MAJOR "

arms.   Every Finlander is liable to military
service, the army consisting of five thousand men
on a peace footing, and thirty-five thousand reserves, only those physically unfit being exempt.
The duration of service is three years with the
colours and two with the reserves, after which

a man is enrolled up to the age of forty years in the militia. The Governor-General of Finland is also Commander-in-Chief, and all commissioned officers must be natives of the Grand Duchy.*

The Finns do not make smart soldiers. They have a slouching, slovenly appearance on parade, more suggestive of sea-boots and sou'-westers than drums and pipeclay; and yet they fought like fiends before Plevna. They are also the finest sailors in the world, although regarded with such superstition that British seamen generally avoid them as shipmates. The occult power over the elements often attributed to Finns was probably originally due to their name, which, like the word "lapp," signifies a wizard.

We parted from most of our friends at Rattijarvi. Only one young lady, residing at Imatrá, accompanied us, together with her brother and a shaggy hound of huge dimensions. "That is Yashka, my sister's lap-dog," said the youth, as the diligence dashed away from the hotel with a clash of yoke bells, and the ungainly creature gambolled after us. "Rather a large one, isn't he?" said my Irish friend, eyeing the dog's ponderous proportions. "Not at all," was his

* A recent Imperial Edict has now cancelled all this.

reply, "quite small"; and the Wicklow man
relapsed into silence, marvelling at the customs
of the country and oblivious of the fact that
Yashka hailed from across the northern border.
"He draws the snowboat," added the Finn, who,
although his knowledge of English was limited,
wished to be communicative. "Ah, yes, the
sledge," replied the Irishman absently, while producing a pipe and a Tauchnitz novel. For a
drive of nearly thirty miles was before us.

And the glorious scenery and bright sunshine
would have been enjoyable enough, but for that
pest of northern latitudes in summer the mosquitos. I have seldom seen them thicker than
on that pine-girt road between Imatrá and
Rattijarvi, even in Alaska, where gold-seekers
aver that this insatiable insect is "as big as a
rabbit and bites at both ends!" The Finland
mosquito is smaller than the Klondiker, but its
bite is quite as poisonous, and we arrived at
our destination with red and swollen faces, for
I had forgotten gloves or a head-net. Nor
was that infallible preventive, essential oil of
cloves,* to be had at Imatrá, where sleep at

* A few drops of this preparation in water on the face and
hands will scare away the most voracious mosquito. But the
application must be frequently renewed.

THE FALLS OF IMATRÄ IN WINTER

To face page 36

night was only obtainable behind a mosquito bar.

The roar of the rapids is audible a good three miles away, but I must confess to a feeling of disappointment on first witnessing the famous falls. This was probably because they had been persistently crammed down my throat on every possible occasion ever since I had set foot in the country. "What do you think of our harbour?" is a question asked every five minutes of the globe-trotter in Sydney. "Of course, you have seen glorious Fujiyama?" says the Jap, and in Finland, "Go to the Falls of Imatrá! They are the finest in the world," is the cry. But they are not the finest in the world—far from it.

In Europe, however, Imatrá is probably unsurpassed, both as regards its grandeur and the stupendous volume of water that rushes down a dark, narrow gorge, formed by precipitous granite cliffs, across which one could fling a pebble and yet fail to hear a steam syren. Lake Saima is nearly one hundred and seventy miles in length, and therefore pours an immense volume of water through the narrow River Vuoksi into Ladoga, the king of European lakes. We pause on the bridge which now spans the falls, once crossed by means of a rope and wicker basket, which,

G

upon one occasion, stuck half-way. The passenger, an unfortunate British tourist, was eventually rescued more dead than alive, after a suspension at a dizzy height of several hours; and his experience must have been a trying one, for even the solid structure on which we stand seems to quiver with the force of the cataract. An English fisherman had a still more exciting escape, for his boat was swept down one of the lesser falls. Strange to say, the skiff was not upset, and its cool and level-headed occupant safely landed his fish in the pool below. Our driver casts a wooden barrel over the parapet, and it is instantly dashed into a thousand pieces against the rocks and boulders that rear their ugly heads above the seething mass of foam and breakers. And yet the actual fall is but forty feet within the space of half a mile, and it is said that the remarkable resonance of Imatrá is due rather to its numerous rocks and channels than to the actual volume of water. Anyhow, it is a grand, impressive sight, especially as we saw it, the pine woods around standing out darkly against a crimson sunset, while below us a seething valley of foam deepened into grey in the twilight. Then suddenly a blaze of electric light was turned on, and the falls flashed like molten silver.

The effect was, perhaps, theatrical, but the scene was as one from fairyland.

Dr. Johnson once remarked that "the finest landscape in the world is nothing without a good inn in the foreground." The worthy doctor would certainly have found Imatrá to his liking, for the comfortable hotel overlooking the falls is one of the best in Finland, which is saying a great deal. The restaurant was crowded, many of its occupants being in evening dress, for this is a fashionable summer resort of the best people in Petersburg. After dinner some strolling musicians enlivened the hours until bedtime, and I listened for the first time to the national instrument of Finland, the "kantele," a kind of zither, which admirably accompanies the wild, weird songs of the country. Finnish music is not unlike Hungarian, and is generally of a sad description, in the minor key. Some of the melodies I heard at Imatrá were very beautiful and charmingly rendered, for Finlanders are born musicians, and musical festivals are frequently held during the summer months in all parts of the country. A number of Finnish songs are published in a volume entitled the *Kanteletar*, and may be procured at any music-shop in Åbo or Helsingfors. The melodies were collected throughout the

length and breadth of Finland by one Elias
Lonrot, who also edited the famous *Kalevala*,
an Iliad of nearly twenty-five thousand verses,
dealing with the history of Finland from the
earliest ages.

Feeling tired after the long day in the open
air, I retired early to rest, but notwithstanding
my luxurious quarters, sleep was out of the
question until the small hours, for the roar of
the rapids was so deafening that a waiting-
room at Clapham Junction, in the busiest part
of the day, would have seemed quiet in comparison with my bedroom at Imatrá. Most of
the guests at the hotel were fishermen, and had
set out the next morning in all directions before
I was stirring. After breakfast I sauntered up
the river with a cigar, to find that my Irish friend
had already managed to fill a respectably-sized
basket with fine trout, some of them over seven
pounds in weight. Finland is unquestionably the
poor fisherman's paradise, for the sport itself
costs him little or nothing. It is only necessary
to obtain permission to fish for salmon or trout,
and the owner will generally grant it free,
or for, at most, a trifling sum. There are
exceptions, however, as at Imatrá, where parts
of the Vuoksi River are preserved by an English

club at Petersburg, who have a cosy cottage
on the spot. Even here, however, the stranger
is always heartily welcomed, and can make sure
of capital sport, for the trout run up to
twenty-five pounds. The best time for the
latter is between the months of June and
September, and good fun can be had with
grayling in July. Salmon are also caught near
Vallinkoski Rapids, some distance below Imatrá,
but the best salmon-fishing is found in the
lakes and rivers of the north. For trout Imatrá
is unsurpassed. It is impossible to fish here
from the bank, but boats can be obtained from
the landlord of the hotel, who also provides
boatmen well acquainted with the river for five
marks a day and a small *pourboire*. The boats
are small and cranky, and only built for two
persons, but accidents are very rare. Most of
the fish are caught in pools between the rapids,
the best places for trout being about a couple
of kilometres above the hotel. A careful selec-
tion of tackle and bait is necessary. Local
fishermen use a light salmon rod with a fine
strong line terminating with a salmon collar,
which should have a trace of fine single grey
gut attached to it. Two or three yards of
collar with swivels should be used, and the

finer the gut the better. No lead is needed except towards sundown, when trolling for the bigger fish in the pools. The best minnows are the "totnes" and "phantom," and dead bait can always be had from the native fishermen in the form of a small salted bleak. They also use a bait of silvered leather, and in the early summer fish with the fly. The "brown palmer" is the best for trout. My Irish friend has since told me that he usually found the early morning and towards sundown the best times of the day for fishing. "Sundown" is here, of course, an elastic term in summer, but, in any case, one must be guided in such matters by the local Izaak Waltons.

A couple of pleasant lazy days brought my stay at Imatrá to a close, and one, a Sunday, was devoted to an excursion to Ruokolaks Church, a few miles distant. The Finns are very devout, and although it often happens that the church is a considerable distance from the dwelling, divine worship on a Sunday, rain or shine, is seldom missed. We found afternoon prayer proceeding, and the sound of voices joining in a simple, melodious hymn tune was wafted to us on the still, pine-scented air. Shortly afterwards the congregation emerged from the old wooden building, some of the women wearing the national costume, with quaint head-dresses and gaily coloured skirts. But the custom is dying out, and this was the only occasion upon which I came across a distinctive native dress during all my wanderings in Finland.

CHAPTER IV

VILLMANSTRAND—NYSLOTT

I HAVE forgotten the name of my hotel at Viborg. It was an exceedingly comfortable, well-managed establishment, and was therefore probably known as the "Societetshuset." Every town of any importance in Finland has its "Societetshuset." Let a stranger be ever so ignorant of the language he has only, on arrival at a wharf or railway station, to tell the cabman to drive to the "Societetshuset," and he will at once be taken to the best hotel in the place.

This useful wrinkle was obtained from a Finnish gentleman, with whom I travelled from Imatrá to Villmanstrand, a pretty little place of some antiquity, for it was founded in 1649. It is now chiefly remarkable for the military manœuvres that take place during the summer, a hydropathic establishment of some renown, and a villa which was built on the shores of Lake Saima for Alexander III. of Russia. As

44

an Imperial residence the house is small, but it was only used on the rare visits of inspection made by the Tsar to the troops of the Grand Duchy. The building is well worth a visit, on account of its purely Finnish architecture, and the fact that it was constructed throughout of the material of the country.*

My Irish friend accompanied me for the first stage of the journey, about three miles by coach, to the landing-stage on Lake Saima. Here the Hibernian bade me farewell to return to his beloved trout, while I embarked on a little steamer for Villmanstrand, a trip of about twenty-five miles, which is made in about three hours, and costs the modest sum of 3 m. 50 p.

On a calm, sunny day this run is delightful, for the water is then as clear as crystal—so clear that one may look over the side and see the shadow of the keel gliding over rocks and sand many fathoms below. The lake is studded with numberless islands, which afford an ever-changing and delightful prospect as we thread our way through a maze of endless and intricate reefs and channels. But the reverse of the picture is not so pleasing, for on dull,

* Permission to view the villa may be obtained of Madame S. Hayren, of Villmanstrand.

gusty days the navigation is too risky to be enjoyable. It can sometimes blow here hard enough (in the words of an old whaling skipper) "to tear a dog's 'ead orf," but the dense mists that occasionally occur in the autumn and blot out familiar landmarks are more dreaded by the skippers of this fresh-water fleet than the wildest gale with a clear sky; for in many parts navigation is accomplished by means of buoys or long poles sunk into the bed of the lake, which become invisible in anything like a fog.

To-day there was no likelihood of such disagreeable contingencies; at least, so I was assured by my travelling acquaintance. He was (like most Finns that I have met) an agreeable companion, full of information, but inquisitive to a degree that in any other nationality would have bordered upon impertinence. "Where is your home?" "Where are you going?" "Are you married?" "Is your wife good-looking?" "Have you any children?" "What is your income?" Such questions are calmly asked in Finland after a five minutes' acquaintance, and the traveller must put up with it as a matter of course. In Helsingfors the income of every inhabitant is published once a year in the newspapers, so that the last inquiry is perhaps only natural. It is only fair to add that in most cases the questioner was only too ready to enlighten one as to the most private details of his own life. I was gratuitously informed (upon this occasion) that my companion was forty-seven years old, that he had twice been married, had seven children (all of them living), and was blessed with an income of about £500 sterling a year derived from a prosperous brewery, to which he was now returning. "And you shall taste of my beer," he added, diving below and returning with a bottle and glasses. "This is some of the best in Finland"; and, indeed, though very light, something like pilsener in colour and consistency, it was excellent, and, be it added, absurdly cheap at something less than fourpence a quart bottle.

The Finn, like the Russian, is generally suspected by those unacquainted with his true character of a strong partiality for strong waters. I allude especially to the lower classes—the Finnish peasantry, whose sobriety is usually regarded in England as being something on a par with that of the Muscovite Moujik. This is surely unjust, for while the importation of alcohol into Finland is strictly prohibited, Government statistics show that its distillers have

decreased during the past twenty years to about
half their original number. In 1870, for instance,
there were no less than sixty factories of alcohol
for human consumption, while in 1897 there were
only thirty-five. The sale of beer, on the other
hand, shows a large increase, for in 1860 only
fifty breweries were in operation throughout the
country. In 1896 there were over a hundred,
and there are now probably more, for brewing
is one of the most prosperous trades of the
country. Sinchykoff, at Helsingfors, is the
Allsopp, and Haltman, of Okenas, the Guinness
of Finland ; and their labels should always be
asked for. The beer is of all kinds—from the
strongest ales to the mildest bock. Haltman's
stout is excellent. There are also in Finland
more than seventy establishments for the manufacture of non-alcoholic beverages, which are
largely consumed by all classes during the summer
months. In face of these facts I refuse to believe
that the Finns are an intemperate race, for in all
my wanderings throughout the country I never
once saw a drunken man until I reached Torneå.
And he was a Swede from South Africa!

New wonders were constantly cropping up in
this land of surprises, but nothing astonished
me more than the freedom with which Finlanders

discussed Russian affairs, Imperial, political, and social, and generally in terms that savoured strongly of treason. This worthy brewer, for instance, openly expressed opinions that, if overheard in Petersburg, would probably have

THE MAN OF MALT

landed him in Schlüsselburg, and this notwithstanding that a party of Russian tourists were sitting well within earshot. A long experience of police *espionnage* in European and Asiatic Russia made me fairly shudder at

H

my friend's temerity, for he expressed his contempt for Muscovite rule in a loud, reckless
tone of voice that finally attracted the notice
of our neighbours. A glance, in our direction,
of surprised annoyance from one of the men
made me still more uneasy, but only egged on
the man of malt. "Look at that woman!" he
cried, as a lady of the group unconsciously
produced a tiny gold case, and lit a dainty
"papirosh." "Do you not call that disgraceful?
Bah! If I caught my wife smoking, I would
shoot her through the head!" At this juncture
the jetty of Villmanstrand was fortunately
reached, and my companion's invectives were
drowned in the bustle of disembarkation. He
landed, much to my surprise, without molestation.
This was not the only occasion upon which I
saw the most extraordinary patience and tolerance shown by Russians towards truculent Finns
—in Finland.

I refused a pressing invitation to visit my
friend's brewery (a day's journey distant),
only to fall into the arms of the Herr Major,
whose tall figure in regimentals was seen surrounded by an admiring circle of the fair sex,
"seeing the boat in," a practice apparently as
popular at Villmanstrand as at Boulogne-sur-

Mer. The Major, who greeted me effusively, would take no denial. To the barracks I must go; so we strolled there together through the quiet streets of the pretty town, with its population of ruddy, white-clad soldiery. Scarcely a civilian was visible, although about 3,000 troops were assembled, many of them under canvas, and I found the barrack-rooms far more cleanly and comfortable than any I had seen in Russia, while the food was distinctly superior. A hearty welcome awaited me at the mess, where champagne was opened in honour of the English guest, and quaffed to a speedy and successful termination of our South African campaign. This, by the way, was the only occasion upon which I met with sympathy for the British arms in the Transvaal. Most Finlanders I came across subsequently (especially in the larger towns) were rabid "pro-Boers," and I heard of at least a score of young men of the better class who had left the Fatherland to join the ranks of President Krüger.

"You will, of course, try Punkaharju," said a young subaltern, my neighbour at the mess table that evening, for the hospitable Major would not hear of my dining at the hotel, a "Societetshuset," as usual! I vaguely smiled

assent, but felt rather doubtful as to whether
"Punkaharju" was the name of a favourite
beverage, an edible luxury, or a game of
chance. The latter was improbable, for cards
and dice are tabooed in most Finnish regiments.
"You should say 'visit,'" said the Major, coming
to the rescue, and correcting his friend's laboured
English, adding, "But of course you will go
there. It is our show place ; you might as well
pass through Naples without seeing Pompeii."

This settled the matter, for time was my
own. And I was grateful, a few hours later,
for the Major's timely advice, notwithstanding
that the journey to the island in question was
accomplished under specially unpleasant conditions. For a steady downpour entailed
imprisonment in a stuffy little cabin, through
the dull portholes of which only flying glimpses
of coast line, wreathed in dense, chilly mist,
were visible. The sky was grey and sodden,
the lake, only yesterday as blue as a sapphire,
now of a dull grey colour, flecked with wavelets
of a dirty drab. Even the pine woods seemed
to droop and shiver in the breeze that moaned
dismally through the rigging, and the lakeside
villas, so bright and attractive in the sunshine,
seemed now bereft of life and gaiety. The

scenery of Finland in fair and foul weather may be likened to a woman, radiantly beautiful in a brilliant ballroom, and emerging sea-sick, sallow, and dishevelled from the horrors of a stormy Channel passage.

Fortunately a short time generally suffices in both cases to restore comely smiles and bright sunshine. Rain in Finland in the early autumn is rare. To-day, however, the flood-gates of heaven seemed to have opened, and the mists lay so thick over the lake that our destination, the old town of Nyslott, was invisible a couple of miles away. But suddenly, as we landed and floundered ankle-deep in mud to the hotel, Nature seemed to dry her eyes, and in an instant the sun had burst forth, dispelling the clouds like magic and streaking the heavens with brilliant blue. The change was like a transformation scene at Covent Garden and in itself well worth the voyage to Finland to witness. I might easily have missed the strange sight, for the regular steamer travels by night from Villmanstrand. I embarked, however, on a special boat, which reached Nyslott early in the afternoon.

Nyslott, in the province of Savolaks, is a fascinating little place, chiefly used as a stepping-

I

stone by those bound for its beautiful neighbour,
Punkaharju.   It is also a favourite resort of
artists on account of its natural surroundings, and
also of antiquarians, who come here from all
parts of Europe to visit its quaint old castle,
while archæologists have also discovered strange
and wonderful relics of the Stone Age in the
neighbourhood.   Finland is rich in antiquities,
and the Helsingfors Museum contains a rare and
marvellous collection of stone, bronze, and iron
weapons which have been brought to light of
recent years, chiefly in the south-western districts.
I myself kicked up a stone spear-head (without
searching for it) while strolling by the lake near
here, and such casual discoveries are frequent
enough.   But let the stranger beware of the
bronze and iron relics sold in the towns, for these,
like the sapphires of Colombo, are frequently
" made in Germany."

At Nyslott I found my first real difficulty with
the language, for not a soul at the hotel (this
time not a well-found " Societetshuset," but a
comfortless inn, yclept the " Auberge de la Poste ")
spoke Russian.   The impossibility of Finnish
lies chiefly in the fact that unless each word is
pronounced with absolute accuracy, you might as
well converse in Patagonian or Chinese, for no

one will understand you. The following notice,
which I found in my bedroom at Nyslott, will
show that the Finnish language can hardly be
called a simple one :—

" Forsumlighet i
upassningen eller annan orsak till missnoje torde
anmatalas till Varden,"

which being interpreted signifies: "Negligence
in service, or other reasons for complaint, should
be notified to the Manager."

Although the food at my auberge savoured of
a Siberian post-house, I staved off the pangs of
hunger with coffee and brown bread and sallied
forth to find a clean and capital restaurant, sug-
gestively named the "Hungerborg," on the
heights overlooking the town. Here I dined
plainly, but well, in a light, cheerful room with a
glorious view of the surrounding country. Also,
the waiter spoke French, which simplified my
study of the usually cryptic bill of fare in which
one item always figured with the regularity of
clockwork—bouillon—with a raw (not the usual
poached) egg served with it. And the former is
a distinct improvement.

I had now adopted Finnish hours. Early
coffee at eight, lunch at ten, dinner at four, and
supper at nine. There was plenty of time, there-

fore, after the meal for a visit to Olofsborg before
sunset, and having obtained, with the assistance
of my French friend, a Russian-speaking guide,
we set out together for the famous castle.   The
latter nearly completely covers a small island,
situated some distance from the shore in the
swiftly flowing Kyrossalmi, a stream connecting
two large lakes to the north and south of Nyslott.
A loud peal at the rusty bell placed for the
purpose at the waterside summons the janitor,
who paddles across in a crazy-looking skiff to
convey us to the castle.   The Kyrossalmi is a
very fair imitation of a torrent, with its eddies
and whirlpools, and we only just manage to
make the landing, and leaping ashore with some
difficulty, stand beneath the frowning portals of
perhaps the most interesting ruin in all Finland.

The castle or fortress of Olofsborg, although
it dates from 1475, is in a remarkable state of
preservation.   The greater part of it looks like
lasting another five centuries, and this although
it has withstood numberless sieges, the effects of
which are still shown by bullet-riddled walls, in
which a few round shot have remained embedded
like currants in a cake.   Many a time has
Olofsborg repelled the hated Muscovite, and
thousands of Finnish patriots have died, bravely

fighting for their country, within its grim grey
walls. In 1742, however, the double-eagle was
triumphantly and permanently unfurled, and the
place for about a century was garrisoned by
Cossacks. In 1847 these were removed, and in
1870 Olofsborg was completely restored by the
State to be handed down to posterity as a silent
record of the glorious deeds wrought by the
Fatherland in defence of its rights and liberty.

Olofsborg was once surrounded by five circular
towers, only three of which are left standing, to
support walls of immense height and thickness.
The lower part of the building, comprising the
portcullis, is of comparatively recent construction,
and although well fortified according to modern
ideas, looks flimsy and tawdry by contrast with
the massive walls of granite in the background.
The dusk is deepening as we cross the threshold
and enter a labyrinth of narrow, dimly lit
passages, which lead into a small, triangular
courtyard open to the sky. Then into outer
darkness once more through low galleries, in
which the custodian strikes a match to disclose
walls glistening with the damp of ages, until a
second open space in the very heart of the
stronghold is reached, a gravelled quadrangle,
surrounded by shrubs and cottage flowers grow-

ing in wild luxuriance around the dwelling-place
of the janitor. His wife sits knitting at an open
doorway in the grey twilight, and a glimpse of
her cosy kitchen, with a kettle singing merrily on
the hob, strikes a snug and cheerful keynote
amid the grim surroundings. The enormous
height of Olofsborg can from here be realised,
and still more so as we painfully clamber up
worn stone steps to the fifth story to obtain a
charming view of Nyslott and an endless vista of
lakes and pine forests darkening against a golden
sunset. Overhead " twilight has let her curtain
down and pinned it with a star," which is joined
every minute by half a dozen other twinkling
worlds. The strong, fresh odour of the pines
arises as the stillness of night creeps over the
land ; only the dull, distant roar of the rapids and
the soft cooing of some pigeons in the dusky
distance are heard, while a number of bats whiz
swiftly past our heads in unpleasant proximity.
We linger, lost in lazy enjoyment of the peaceful
scene, until the lights of Nyslott shine out, one
by one, like glowworms in the dusky distance.
It is time to return. As we descend, " Vot eto
tiourma !" ("There is the prison !") suddenly
cries my guide, pointing to a low doorway sunk
deep into the masonry. A flight of stone steps

leads down into an invisible cavern, whence issues a damp, musty odour. The place is suggestive of mediæval deeds of darkness, and a number of rats scutter away at our approach. Here, in the good old days, unhappy wretches were bricked up alive to expire in agony from starvation and want of air. In

OLOFSBORG

another dungeon ring bolts are still shown, to which prisoners were secured while undergoing torture by fire, steel, and the lash.

We retrace our steps past innumerable passages, with which the old structure is honeycombed. I am told that a subterranean passage leads under the river to the town of Nyslott, and although not anxious to explore its depths,

can well believe it. By the time we reach
it the chapel is in darkness, and I survey its
gloomy, ghostlike interior by the aid of a candle.
It is a bare, unlovely edifice. All creeds have
worshipped here—Catholic, Lutheran, and Greek,
which constitutes the chief interest connected
with the sacred building. A hideous pulpit with
a huge sounding-board recalls old-fashioned
Protestant churches in rural England, and the
altar is dilapidated, but not picturesque. There
are some pictures—crude, vulgar daubs—but the
janitor draws my attention to them with as much
pride and care as though he were exhibiting
masterpieces of Rubens or Murillo.

Madame presents me with a sweet-smelling
nosegay as I recross the courtyard, and re-
luctantly permits her chubby-cheeked little boy
to accept a mark in exchange. Finland is one
of the few countries in Europe (with the exception, perhaps, of France) where the peasantry
do not invariably expect remuneration for an act
of courtesy involving a trifling cost. And so
homewards, across the ferry, and through the
silent streets to the auberge, now sleeping in the
starlight, for we are early folks in Nyslott. I
shake off my guide with some difficulty, for a
glass of " vodka " with the janitor has inspired

him with conviviality and wild projects for the morrow. At length he departs, and I seek the damp sheets of my narrow couch to dream of men in armour, dismal dungeons, and dainty damosels. During the greater part of the night, however, I lie awake, bitterly realising that there are even less agreeable bedfellows in this world than the much-abused mosquito!

CHAPTER V

PUNKAHARJU—SAINT MICHEL

THE map of Finland in outline is, as has been shown, an almost exact presentment of a female dancing (according to patriotic Finns) a derisive "Fandango." Hold the atlas a short distance away, and it will appear as though a quantity of ink had been spilt by some clumsy partner over the lady's skirt, sadly disfiguring it from the waist downwards, although the bodice of the gown has, comparatively speaking, escaped injury. The blue stains are the bewildering maze of inland seas and rivers, which have gained for Finland her pseudonym of "The Land of a Thousand Lakes." It will be seen that this hydrographic puzzle occurs chiefly in the south. Lapland (as represented by the lady's bodice), although a well-watered country, is, by comparison, an arid desert.

It is no exaggeration to say that one may take a canoe, embark, say at Viborg, and travel at

a fair rate of speed for fifty consecutive days
without revisiting the same spot, or once beaching
the boat. I cannot conceive a more enjoyable
trip for the keen fisherman with a taste for outdoor life, whose means do not run to rights on
a river in Scotland or Norway. The whole
"programme" (fishing included) has been carried
out, to the writer's knowledge, for under £30,
commencing and ending at Liverpool Street.
Where in Europe can you find such excellent
sport at such a trifling cost? A word of advice,
though, from "a friend who knows." "Take
your canoe out from England," for the local
"Rob-Roy" is a weirdly-built contrivance, which
generally entails more toil than pleasure on its
occupant.

The characteristic patience and energy of the
Finlander are nowhere more clearly shown than
by the marvellous results he has attained by connecting and utilising the natural waterways of his
country. Remote and barren districts in the
interior have leapt into life and activity, and vast
tracts of useless country have been reclaimed,
since a steam syren first echoed through once
lonely wastes, now occupied by thriving towns
and prosperous factories. The innovation has furthered not only mercantile interests, for churches,

schools, and even universities in many parts of the interior owe their existence to those who first conceived the idea of cleaving navigable canals, thus uniting this huge network of lakes and rivers once separated from each other by impassable marsh and trackless forest.

The earliest attempts date from the Middle Ages, and ruined and abandoned dykes and ditches of great antiquity still exist in various parts of Finland. As early as the twelfth century a commercial water-road existed from Lake Ladoga across the whole country, running in a north-westerly direction up to Uleåborg, on the Gulf of Bothnia—a primitive route this, with, of course, frequent intervals of land. To realise the magnitude of the work as it stands the reader must realise the hydrography of southern Finland; and this may be divided into three parts or districts: (1) the eastern section, comprising a hundred and twenty large lakes and some hundreds of smaller ones; (2) the central division, including Nyslott and Punkaharju, and consisting of six hundred and fifty lakes of various sizes, and innumerable marshes; and (3) the western district, which is of higher altitude than the other, and the streams of which are rendered less navigable by reason of torrents and rapids.

The motive power, however, afforded by the latter for the use of factories and saw-mills amply compensates for a comparatively small water-traffic.

The first really successful works were accomplished between 1835 and 1838, when canals were cut connecting Lakes Kanhevesi and Kallavesi. The first inland steamer (a locally-built, very primitive craft) was launched on Lake Saima in 1833, but it was only twelve years later that this lake was made navigable from Villmanstrand to Insalmi, a distance of about three hundred kilometres. A project to open up navigation between the sea coast and the interior had long been under consideration, and the Emperor Nicholas I. himself displayed a keen and personal interest in the scheme, which had for a long period been considered impracticable. In 1845, however, work was commenced in real earnest, and eleven years later the Saima Canal, one of the greatest engineering feats of the nineteenth century, was an accomplished fact. Financially, it is a huge success. In 1897, for instance, 5,198 steamships and sailing-vessels passed through with passengers and merchandise, and this notwithstanding that the railway was then open to many parts of the north-eastern district, formerly only

K

attainable by post-road or water. In no other
instance has it been possible to connect the lake
system with either the Gulfs of Bothnia or
Finland. An ineffectual attempt was made some
years ago to connect Lake Pajanne, an important
centre of traffic in the central district, with the
Gulf of Finland by means of the Kymmene River,
but this project, owing to its enormous expense,
was soon abandoned. The commercial importance of Pajanne, which drains two large lakes
and their numberless tributaries, soon suggested
another plan, viz. the construction of the Vesi-
jarvi Canal, which now connects the steamboat
traffic direct with a large station on the Finland
Railway. The crafty Finn is not to be beaten—
when he cannot reach the sea, he finds a railway!

It would weary the reader to quote other and
innumerable instances where an infinite expenditure of patience, skill, and labour have been
brought to bear upon the development of water-
communication throughout the Grand Duchy.
Suffice it to say that there are now very few lakes
in Southern Finland (even the smallest) without
a regular service of well-found steamboats, where
the traveller will find every comfort at a more
than moderate price (he can have a private cabin
and champagne with his meals, if so disposed)

and civility from all. The entire expenditure up to the present time on the waterways of Finland amounts to about twenty-five million marks,* and it costs about another 250,000 marks for the maintenance of canals, payment of officials, etc. The receipts, on the other hand, are very considerable, especially those from the Saima Canal.†

There is a good post-road from Nyslott to Punkaharju, a distance of about eighteen miles, and on a fine day the drive is said to be a pleasant one. Being of a lazy disposition, however, and preferring a well-cooked *déjeuner* to black bread and dubious eggs (to say nothing of mosquitos), I chose the boat. The captain, who was attired in evening clothes and a tall hat (a summer garb apparently popular amongst these fresh-water skippers), effusively welcomed me for the sole and simple reason that I was an Englishman, and invited me to take my " smorgasbord" in his snug little cabin beneath the bridge. Here was no "pro-Boer," at any rate.

* This does not include Ostro-Bothnia, or the lakes and rivers of the north.

† The Russian Government has lately had under consideration a waterway from the Gulf of Finland to the White Sea in the Far North. The project (proposed by a Monsieur Timonsoff) is now approved of by the authorities, and the new canal, which is to serve both strategic and commercial purposes, will probably be commenced this summer (1901).

Krüger should be hanged to the nearest tree, his
people should be exterminated to a man, the
insults offered to the British nation must be
expiated by the absolute annexation of the
Transvaal—lock, stock, and barrel.   On these

A FRESH-WATER "SALT"

points the skipper was adamant, but became
somewhat vague after his third go of "branvinn."
"Tell me! What was all the quarrel about?"
he asked, absently munching a caviare sandwich.
"Is Krüger really the rascal they make him out

to be in England?" I sadly changed the subject, for patience has its limits.

The little steamer was crowded, for in fine weather Punkaharju is a favourite resort, not only of tourists, but of the good people of Nyslott. There is something very Gallic about the way in which the Finns take their pleasure —a kind of spontaneous gaiety not generally associated with the cool and stolid northerner. If you want to please a Finlander, call him a "Frenchman of the North," and it is no misnomer, for the merry little parties that I saw to-day picnicking in the shady woods around Punkaharju recalled Sundays at Asnières or Bougival. Finland is well out of the track of the British tourist, and this was the solitary occasion upon which I came across any of my compatriots. Paterfamilias was there—all guidebook and pugaree; his son, a supercilious youth from Oxford, and three angular daughters, who moved vaguely about in rows. The latter were attired in hard straw hats (no veils), coloured blouses, and dingy black skirts—a terrible combination, usually adopted for some occult reason by the Englishwoman abroad. I have been told that it is "neat and inexpensive." As for the neatness—save the mark! But economical

L

reasons could surely suggest a less hideous costume than one that renders even a pretty woman grotesque in the eyes of a foreigner.

A frugal lunch at a snug little inn was followed by one of my most enjoyable days in Finland, for the heat was tempered by a cool breeze, and the lights and shadows cast by lazily drifting cloudlets enhanced the calm, peaceful beauty of

"NEAT AND INEXPENSIVE"

the island. The Herr Major had rightly described Punkaharju as the " Pearl of Lakes," for Switzerland itself could scarcely produce a more entrancing prospect. Imagine a long, low island, or rather a succession of islands forming one uninterrupted stretch of park and meadowland nearly six miles in length. So narrow is Punkaharju that in places a pebble can be thrown

PUNKAHARJU

To face page 70

across it from one beach to another, while in other parts it widens into charming glades and valleys where ferns grow knee-deep and the grass is carpeted with wild flowers. From a distance the place presents almost the appearance of a viaduct, so steep are its cliffs, which arise abruptly to a height of a hundred feet from the blue waters of Lake Puruvesi. From the narrow ridge at the summit you may obtain one of the finest views in Finland, and realise by looking down the almost perpendicular slope on either side the quaint natural formation of the island, probably due to some convulsion of nature. For the top of Punkaharju is almost razor-like, and to this is due its name, which signifies, literally, "hog's-back." The best time to visit this lovely spot is the fall of the year, for the forests are then flecked with the bronze and golden tints of dying leaves, which relieve to a certain extent the monotonous vista of every shade of verdure that meets the eye in summer. The islands are, of course, thickly wooded (most places are in Southern Finland), but the Finn has made the most of his opportunities, and cunningly-contrived alleys and avenues in the network of branches and greenery afford delightful glimpses of lake, forest, and field, and there

are comfortable seats at short intervals where
the wayfarer may contemplate the beauties of
nature. Above all, should you visit this place
in autumn, don't miss the sunset, for it is one
of the sights of Finland. But Punkaharju is

"A TWEED-CLAD FIGURE APPROACHED"

beautiful at any time — in summer, smiling
in the midst of flowers, and even in winter,
shrouded in deep snow and lashed by the pitiless
storms that sweep down from the north. For
even at this inclement season there are quiet,
still days, when the sky is like a turquoise, and

sleigh bells jingle merrily over the frozen lake while the snow-clad little island sparkles like a diamond in the sunshine.

It was twilight as I made my way homeward, leaving the glorious sunset that still lingered in broad streaks of crimson dully reflected in the steel-grey lake. As I neared the hotel a tweed-clad figure approached me. " Don't bathe," it said, and I recognised the youth from Oxford, who, it appeared, had been nearly drowned that afternoon in one of the deep and dangerous eddies off the island. I had no intention of bathing, but mention this fact for the benefit of those who, like my friend, may be tempted on a hot summer's day to take a dip in cool and alluring Puruvesi.

Two routes now lay before me to Helsingfors : the one by which I had come *viâ* Villmanstrand, and the other *viâ* Mikkeli (or, as it is sometimes called, St. Michel), from both of which towns it is an easy journey to the capital by railway. I chose Mikkeli (about ten hours by steamer from Nyslott), a pretty, sleepy little town, which I reached early one morning only to find that the one train of the day had departed. Natural surroundings here are the sole attraction, for Mikkeli is one of the modern mushroom-like towns that have sprung up by the side of the Helsingfors-Kuopio railway. I found a primitive little restaurant, however, in some shady gardens where one could breakfast and dine in the open, and where I dawdled away the day pleasantly enough until nightfall brought the welcome whistle of the mail train.

It might have been worse, for Mikkeli was at its best, and in holiday garb on the occasion of some national feast. The restaurant was gaily decorated with bunting, paper lanterns dangled from the trees in anticipation of an illumination, and the tables around mine were occupied from midday until dusk by merry groups of people with their gaily dressed women-folk and a sprinkling of the military from a neighbouring garrison town. During the afternoon a band enlivened the proceedings and a brisk trade was done by neatly clad waitresses in coffee and cakes, foaming bocks, and an amber-coloured beverage comprising wild strawberries and crushed ice. I found the latter consisted of "mjod" and a cunning mixture of liqueurs—a seductive and apparently innocent drink, of which, however, one might easily take too much on a hot summer's day. My stock of tobacco being exhausted, I purchased, for the first time

(with some misgivings), a Finnish cigar. To
my surprise the tobacco, though somewhat
coarse, was excellent and the cigar absurdly
cheap at about $2\frac{1}{2}d$. A few days later, at Helsingfors, I bought some cigars at the factory
of Borgstrom and Co., at 25 marks a hundred,
which would certainly have fetched $8d$. apiece
in Bond Street. I mention this fact in order
that smokers may save themselves the expense
of bringing their own tobacco into Finland.
Cigarettes are also largely manufactured in Åbo
and Helsingfors, and sold throughout the country,
but they are very inferior to, although quite as
dear as, the Russian "papirosh," while exorbitant
prices are asked for genuine Egyptians. Most
of the tobacco employed in Finland for cigar
manufacture is imported from Germany. "Three
Castles" and Wills's "Capstan Navy Cut"
tobaccos may be obtained in most of the
principal towns, but the Finns are not great
pipe-smokers.

As I left towards nine o'clock for the railway station, preparations were being made for
an impromptu dance. Lights sparkled from
the dark pines, and now and again a rocket
would shoot into the starry heavens, to fall in
a shower of diamonds over the lake. It

was a pretty, homely scene, and although the
gaiety was unrestrained, it was almost childlike
in its nature and absolutely devoid of any
objectionable feature. A snugly lit compartment
and snowy sheets awaited me, and I turned into
bed not sorry, after all, to have wasted a day at
Mikkeli in such pleasant company.

CHAPTER VI

A RETROSPECT

" HOW little you English know of my country and its history !" was the remark of a Finnish telegraph official, who had lived in London, and whose acquaintance I made in the beer gardens at Mikkeli. He was quite right. For some reason or another this wonderful little land is seldom heard of or even read about in England, where it is generally regarded by the majority of people as a mere unit of the Russian Empire, devoid of political and social interest, and chiefly remarkable for a yearly contribution of timber to the markets of Europe. Personally I must own to the densest ignorance on the subject before my visit. Many a time in British seaports have I watched some clumsy, weather-beaten barque from the eastern shores of the Baltic discharge her cargo, and pictured her return to some squalid, desolate settlement in the Far North, never dreaming that she had sailed away from a crowded city with stone buildings and boulevards, tramcars, and electric light!

While rolling luxuriously towards Helsingfors, let us glance briefly at the trials and crises which Finland has endured to emerge, notwithstanding almost insuperable difficulties, one of the most enlightened and civilised little countries in Europe. I will not enter into lengthy historical details, which would be out of place in these sketchy notes of travel, but merely try to give a short outline of the history of the Grand Duchy from the Swedish era up to the present day.

Finland from the darkest ages has had to contend against the cupidity of two powerful neighbours, Russia and Sweden. Many Finns will tell you that they were happier and more prosperous under Swedish rule, but if Russia were expelled to-morrow by another power, or even if Sweden were to reoccupy the country, it is probable that discontent would still prevail. For the Finn, like the Irishman, is hard to please in the matter of government, and no wonder. A lad of eighteen generally objects to wearing Eton jackets!

The period at which Finland was first populated is doubtful, although archæological discoveries pertaining to the Bronze and Iron Ages show that the country was then inhabited by a people who pursued cattle - rearing and worked mines yielding copper and gold. We will not go so far back, however, but start from the twelfth century, when Finland was definitely annexed by King Eric of Sweden and paganism was succeeded by Christianity. For many years the Finns enjoyed the same rights and privileges as their conquerors, but this golden era was followed by a long reign of oppression, and it would seem as though this unfortunate country had been doomed to pass for ever through intermediate stages of servile subjection and comparative liberty.

The year 1473 witnessed the first important Russian invasion of the eastern frontier, a struggle lasting many years, in which thousands on both sides perished. It was during this campaign that the castle of Olofsborg was built to repel the invaders, who were finally defeated after a desperate attack on the city of Viborg in 1497. But Finland only escaped the Muscovite yoke to fall into the hands of the tyrant Christian II. of Denmark, who, conquering Sweden three years later, instituted a reign of · terror, which was happily only of short duration. For, three years later, Gustavus Vasa had routed the Danes and reinstated Swedish rule.

Finland enjoyed, under Gustavus I., a much-needed period of peace and prosperity. Civilisation attained a stage hitherto unknown in her annals, and the country made rapid strides in the hands of the great reformer. Agriculture especially improved, and the desert provinces of Tavastland and Savolax were reclaimed and colonised by a thrifty and thriving population. Finally, in 1550, the ancient city of Helsingfors (on the River Wanda, some four miles from the modern capital) was founded, a decade prior to the death of one of the wisest and most tolerant rulers that Finland has ever known.

But fresh troubles were in store, and in 1570 war broke out afresh with Russia; this time, however, with the Baltic provinces as a battle-field, although Finland—utilised by Sweden as a base of operations—was more than once invaded. On this occasion the Swedes were again victorious, but peace was only concluded after a harassing campaign of many years' duration. Only a year afterwards Finland was fated to experience the horrors of a civil war, which, however, came as a blessing in disguise; for the reigning monarch was deposed by Charles IX., who proved a second Gustavus, and who is known to this day among the peasantry as "Charles the Good."

Finland now enjoyed a whole century of peace and progression, during which the reign of Queen Christine (the Good Queen Bess of Finland) is the most memorable ; for it is associated with two great events — the founding of the University of Åbo* and the removal of the ancient city of Helsingfors, on the River Wanda, to its present site on the Gulf of Finland. Important reforms also took place in the administration of the government, while the modes of communication throughout the country were greatly improved. The war of 1700 (which lasted more than twenty years and was brought about by Charles XII. of glorious memory) was perhaps the most disastrous of any, for Finland, drained of all her available fighting men for the Swedish Army, was thus left at the mercy of Russia. The country was raided from end to end, and thousands of all ages and both sexes were carried off to Russia and there sold as slaves to even Persian taskmasters, for in 1726 over a thousand unhappy Finns were living in bondage at Ispahán. The "Great Northern War" will

* Transferred to Helsingfors in 1828.

M

long be remembered as the most terrible that
was ever waged in a land that may well be called
the "Kingdom of Zeus"!

In 1808 the final and decisive struggle took
place, by which Finland was wrested for ever
from the Swedes. The country had never been
so prosperous, for during the reign of Gustavus IV.
(the last Swedish monarch) education, commerce,
agriculture, and even art were at their zenith.
The Finns themselves were satisfied, and asked
for no better form of government, when, like a
bolt from the blue, the Russians crossed the
eastern frontier, on that fatal 21st February, 1808,
without even declaring war. It was almost a
bloodless conquest, for the invaders were march-
ing under the threatening shadow of the great
Napoleon; and the army of Finland, deserted
and disorganised, fled before them northwards in
dismay. A Russian occupation of the southern
coast followed. Helsingfors was occupied after
its hitherto impregnable fortress of Sveaborg
had been basely surrendered, without firing a
shot, by Johan Cronstedt, whose name is still
reviled as a traitor by patriotic Swedes. In
vain were Tammerfors and Kuopio stubbornly
defended by the gallant little garrisons of Adler-
kreutz and Von Dobeln; the panic-stricken

Swedes had fled, leaving them to their fate. Nevertheless some remarkable instances of Finnish bravery are recorded, notably at the battle of Oravais, where 8,500 Russians were held in check by a third of their number for fourteen hours; and it was only owing to a reinforcement of 2,000 men that the former were at last victorious. No invasion was ever resisted with such dogged tenacity, or at such fearful odds, for what was this handful of undrilled peasantry against the mighty legions of the Tsar? The campaign could have but one ending. In September, 1809, Finland, including the Åland Islands, was ceded to Russia, and the River Torneå, at the head of the Gulf of Bothnia, fixed as the Swedish boundary-line.

Such is a brief history of Finland up to the time of the Russian annexation. Let us see what has happened since.

It is an incontestable fact that holy Russia generally contrives to "Russianise" the countries she annexes in an incredibly short space of time. Take, for instance, Poland, where the national language has become practically obsolete; or the recently acquired provinces in Central Asia, where Merv and Bokhara have been converted into tawdry modern towns, bereft of all their

Eastern charm and originality. Russian is now spoken in the bazaars, swarming with drab-coated Cossacks, barrack-like buildings abound, vodka has replaced sherbet, and the mosques and minarets of Islam are outnumbered by the golden domes and crosses of the Greek faith. In the east, as in the west, the nationality, language, and even religion of the conquered races are slowly expiring in the iron grip of the Bear. "The mills of the Tsar grind slowly, but they grind exceeding small"!

In the case of Finland it has been different, at any rate for nearly a century, although a change is at hand. For Alexander I., immediately after the conquest of the country, proposed a political programme which was universally welcome throughout the Grand Duchy. Briefly, it came to this: That Finland was to maintain absolutely the same freedom and independence that she had enjoyed under Swedish rule. The internal government of the country would still be administered by its people, who would continue to frame its laws, while the religion and language would never be interfered with. The Emperor simply reserved the right to act as Commander-in-Chief of the army and direct the management of foreign affairs. Otherwise Finland was to remain an independent state, protected rather than governed by her powerful neighbour.

So far as the Alexanders were concerned, these promises were faithfully fulfilled, although the reign of Nicholas I. cast a temporary shadow over the prosperous days upon which Finland had fallen since her Russian alliance. The Iron Tsar could not understand that to transplant a tree it is necessary to uproot it by gentle rather than forcible means. The Finns had not only become civilised by contact with the Swedes, but had been imbued with many of their characteristics only to be eliminated by time and tolerance. The liberty also which they had enjoyed under Alexander I. led them to expect the same clemency and consideration from his successor ; but a grievous disappointment was the result. Although Nicholas could not openly violate the constitutional liberty granted to Finland, he did his utmost to restrict it by binding, both intellectually and commercially, the progress of the country. Many schools were closed, public speaking and the Press subjected to the severest censure, while the Diet was not once convoked during this reign of thirty years. Had Nicholas I. lived another decade he would probably have deprived Finland, fifty years ago,

N

of the rights and privileges only lately withdrawn by his illustrious namesake. But this evil day was postponed by the accession in 1855 of Alexander II., whose coronation was naturally viewed at first with some apprehension and distrust. That happier days were in store for Finland was soon, however, shown by the new ruler's first act, which was to convoke the Finnish Parliament after its long period of enforced inactivity, and to open it in person, pointedly addressing its members in the French language. This in itself restored a confidence which was not misplaced, for during the reign of this monarch the fears of Finland were lulled into security. The country conclusively proved her ability for self-government, for rapid progress was soon made in every sphere of development. The exports increased yearly, agriculture improved, factories were founded, railways and canals constructed, and the telegraph carried to the most remote districts. The liberty of the Press, withheld by Nicholas, was restored, while public education was furthered by the founding of board schools in the smaller towns and villages. The independence of his nationality, so dear to the Finn, was doubly cemented by a commercial treaty with Russia and the establishment of a customs tariff on the frontier. No Russian Tsar was ever so beloved and respected as Alexander II., and his tragic death in 1881 was universally and deeply deplored throughout Finland.

Alexander III. continued to carry out the policy of non-interference in Finnish affairs, for the reign of his predecessors had shown not only that the Finns could be trusted to govern themselves, but that tactful treatment was capable of converting them into loyal and devoted subjects. The conspicuous bravery of the Finnish troops before Plevna had shown that, notwithstanding their race, religion, and language, the Finns were willing to fight, and fight loyally, for a Tsar who respected their rights and privileges. And the assurances of his predecessors were solemnly renewed by Nicholas II., the first period of whose reign entitled him to be regarded for some years as a friend and benefactor. Few people in the Grand Duchy foresaw the fatal result of the Diet convoked by the Tsar towards the end of 1898 to discuss a project whereby Finland was to provide a yearly contingent of several thousand men to serve in the garrisons of Russia proper. A bombshell falling in the House of Assembly would have scared its members less than this

demand, which, from a Finnish standpoint, was
little short of outrageous. For the army of
Finland had hitherto been regarded by Finlanders as a purely national institution, as
independent of the Russian War Office as the
army of the Kaiser itself. A staunch ally
Finland had always proved herself, but one to
be led, not driven. The Finns had never up till
this period served under Russian officers, and
were only bound by law to furnish a military
force for the defence of their own country. The
proposal was, as usual, put to the vote, and
unanimously rejected.

His Majesty the Tsar was, it is said, himself
unwilling to press the matter further. But the
Governor-General of Finland and other Russian
ministers were indefatigable in their endeavours
to find a loophole out of the difficulty. How
this was done is a mystery. The fact remains
that on the 15th February, 1899, the manifesto
was issued, which practically deprived Finland
of her independence. A glance at the procla-
mations respectively issued by Alexander I. at
the commencement, and Nicholas II. at the end,
of the century will show what a death-blow the
latter monarch, with one stroke of the pen, has
dealt to the liberties of Finland.

"It is necessary for the welfare of Finland," says the latest document, "that she be united by closer bonds to the Empire of Russia. The Diet will be abolished, having ceased to be essential to the government of the country. His Majesty Nicholas II. will in future legislate for Finland without the latter's advice or assistance, and every new law must henceforth be passed for the Grand Duchy by the Imperial Council at Petersburg, and must be sanctioned, before its enforcement, by the Emperor. On the other hand, a certain number of Finnish Senators (appointed by the Russian President) will be entitled to a vote in the proceedings." Other less important clauses follow, all pointing to one end and object—the abolishment of self-government for Finland.

The manner in which the Finns received the Tsar's announcement was as characteristic of these quiet, homely people as it was pathetic. On the Sunday following Helsingfors was a city of mourning. There was no violent protest, no rioting in the streets, merely a silent, resigned attitude amongst all classes, infinitely more pitiful to witness than a hostile demonstration. Only a week before the streets of the bright little city were crowded with happy, contented

people, church bells were pealing merrily,
military bands were playing in the parks,
and the blue harbour was alive with launches
and white-sailed pleasure yachts. What a contrast to this Sunday of despair, when every
man, woman, and child were in mourning, and
the very buildings were draped in black crape!
In the evening all places of amusement were
closed by common consent, while the tolling of
bells and deserted streets likened Helsingfors to
a plague-stricken city. The most striking event
of that melancholy day was towards dusk, when
a dense crowd assembled round the statue of
Alexander II. in the Senate Square. Here the
national air of Finland was sung by thousands,
as closely veiled women and children laid
wreaths and flowers in touching appeal towards the living, at the feet of the dead, Tsar,
who had loved and governed Finland so well.
And in every town and village throughout the
country the same scenes were enacted. Centuries
of servility had rendered the Finn too submissive
to rebel. He could only humbly appeal for
justice and the restoration of the rights of which
his fatherland had been so suddenly bereft.

The Tsar's refusal to receive a petition presented shortly after these events clearly proved

that all endeavours to obtain a remission of the
manifesto would be useless. Several hundred
copies of the address were specially inscribed
by the ladies of Helsingfors, and despatched
throughout the country to the very heart of Lapland itself for signatures, of which no less than
half a million were obtained in under a month.
" The nation herself will appeal to the Tsar!"
was the message that was flashed over Finland,
awakening hope on all sides. Meetings were
held everywhere in cities, villages, and hamlets.
Where no halls were available, churches were
thrown open, and men and women crowded
eagerly to sign copies of the address. The
literate only were permitted to affix their names,
which gave rise to many touching incidents.
In one village of the far north an old man of
seventy came to his master and begged that
he might be taught to write his name. " Am
I not to be allowed to take part in the protest ?"
argued the old peasant, with tears trickling down
his furrowed cheeks, and it was only after an
hour's hard work that he was consoled by being
able to scrawl his name in illegible characters.
Others in remote districts sought the parish
schoolmaster, and came back proudly when,
by dint of perseverance, they also were able

to become signatories. In a certain instance the owner of a farm in the far north learnt from one of his labourers, who had been south, what was being done. It was too far for all the people on his farm to travel to the nearest village where signatures were being received, but the farmer was not disheartened by this. He sat down and wrote to the Emperor himself, imploring him to repeal his manifesto. The document, having been signed by everyone in the place, was then sent by special messenger, and eventually reached its destination!

The most northern settlement to be visited by an emissary was Rovaniemi, within the Polar Circle. In this district snow-shoes (in winter) are the only mode of communication. It was deemed impossible at Helsingfors to procure any signatures north of this, but the Rovaniemi peasants were equal to the task. The best runner of the district volunteered to cover more than a hundred miles, through desolate wilds, in order to reach a place still further north, Kittilä. He had but twenty-four hours in which to complete the journey, but it was accomplished in eighteen, speeding over frozen swamp and through dense forest at a pace that would have killed a man less imbued with patriotic ardour. At Kittilä runners on ski were despatched in all directions, and in a few hours more than seventy men had come in to the village from marvellous distances at incredible speed. A meeting was held, and a document signed, which was at once despatched to Helsingfors. One bearer had to travel on foot over a hundred miles, another thirty miles on horseback and a hundred and fifty miles more by sleigh to reach the railway. But the feat was accomplished, and the Kittilä petition found its way with the rest to the feet of the Emperor.

A deputation of five hundred peasants from the same number of parishes proceeded to Petersburg, but only disappointment awaited the delegates, some of whom had accomplished long and perilous sleigh journeys in order to lay the prayer of their countrymen before the " Great White Tsar "! His Majesty was unable to grant them an audience, for reasons best known to the Imperial Council. Thus the dispirited messengers sadly returned to their distant homes (some of them within the Arctic Circle), for the fate of Finland was now sealed.

A Russian official of distinction recently informed me that in his opinion Nicholas II. has really conferred a benefit upon the Grand Duchy by uniting it more closely politically, if not socially, with the mother country. The liberty of the Finns must, of course, suffer, but, added my friend, "the mere fact of a small state of under three million souls retaining its independence while Poland herself is resigned to Muscovite rule is an anomaly that could no longer be tolerated." "But Finland must eventually become completely absorbed," I urged. "She has already lost her liberty—the religion and language must follow in time." "What of that ?" replied the Russian. "She will gain in civilisation and commerce by closer intercourse with us. And, after all, what are a paltry three millions amongst over a hundred and twenty ?"

Intelligent Finns (and there are many) will argue that this is all nonsense ; that Russia, with all her wealth and power, has not yet attained the civilisation to be found throughout the little land of Suomi. The intelligence, they will urge, of even the most illiterate Finnish peasant as compared with that of the Russian Moujik is a proof of this. Commerce is an open question, but surely the education of the country must eventually suffer under an empire in which schools are often sacrificed in order that dramshops may flourish? " As for our system of government," concludes the Finn, ": can you compare it with one notoriously rotten to the core ?"

The reader will kindly note that it is a Finn (and not the author) who speaks, for, personally, I am of opinion that this matter is one for settlement by Russia alone, and that the interference, therefore, of other nations savours strongly of impertinence.

As usual, there is much to be said on both sides, but although Russia has unquestionably gained, by conquest, the right of legislation over her Grand Duchy, I question, as a humble and superficial observer, whether the Imperial Government will eventually derive advantage from coercing, and thereby estranging, a peaceable people who, so long as they were left alone, were loyal and devoted subjects. During my wanderings through Finland I have met and conversed with all classes—from wealthy merchants in Helsingfors to wood-cutters in the forests of the far north—and the cry has always been the same : " What have we done that our constitution should be taken from us ?" " Was Finland ever more prosperous and contented than she has been under Home Rule ?" " We only demand our rights and privileges. It is surely little enough that we ask for, after all!"

> "O leave us our little margins, waste ends of land and sea,
> A little grass, and a hill or two, and a shadowing tree;
> O leave us our little rivers, that sweetly catch the sky,
> To drive our mills, and to carry our wood, and to ripple by."*

Will the prayer remain unanswered?

* *The Cry of the Little Peoples*, by RICHARD LE GALLIENNE.

CHAPTER VII

A FEW FACTS ABOUT FINLAND

"WHAT sort of a place is Finland?" asked a friend whom I met, on my return from that country, in London. "Very much the same as Lapland, I suppose? Snow, sleighs, and bears, and all that kind of thing?"

My friend was not singular in his ideas, for they are probably those of most people in England. At present Finland is a *terra incognita*, though fortunately not likely to remain one. Nevertheless, it will probably take years to eradicate a notion that one of the most attractive and advanced countries in Europe, possessed in summer of the finest climate in the world, is not the eternal abode of poverty, cold, and darkness. It was just the same before the railway opened up Siberia and revealed prosperous cities, fertile plains, and boundless mineral resources to an astonished world. A

decade ago my return from this land of civilisation, progress, and, above all, humanity was
invariably met by the kind of question that
heads this chapter, with the addition, as a rule,
of facetious allusions to torture and the knout!
My ignorance, however, of Finland as she really
is was probably unsurpassed before my eyes were
opened by a personal inspection, so I cannot
afford to criticise.

What is Finland, and what are its geographical and climatic characteristics? I will try to
answer these questions briefly and clearly without
wearying the reader with statistics. In the first
place, Finland (in Finnish, " Suomi ") is about the
size of Great Britain, Holland, and Belgium
combined, with a population of about two and
a half millions. Its southern and western shores
are washed by the Baltic Sea, while Lake Ladoga
and the Russian frontier form the eastern boundary. Finland stretches northward far beyond
the head of the Gulf of Bothnia, where it joins
Norwegian territory, but the head of the imaginary female I have already described (which
forms the northern extremity) does not touch
the Arctic Ocean. There are thirty-seven towns,
of which only seven have a population exceeding
ten thousand, viz. Helsingfors, Åbo, Tammer-

fors, Viborg, Uleàborg, Vasa (Nikolaistad), and
Bjorneborg.

Finland is essentially a flat country, slightly
mountainous towards the north, but even her
highest peak (Haldesjock, in Finnish Lapland) is
under four thousand feet in height.   South of this
a hill of three hundred feet is called a mountain ;
therefore Alpine climbers have no business here.
The interior may be described as an undulating
plateau largely composed of swamp and forest,
broken with granite rocks and gravel ridges and
honeycombed with the inland waters known as
" The Thousand Lakes " (although ten thousand
would be nearer the mark), one of which is three
times the size of the Lake of Geneva.   The
rivers are small and unimportant, the largest
being only about the size of the Seine.   On the
other hand, the numerous falls and rapids on
even the smallest streams render their ascent in
boats extremely difficult and often impossible.
But lakes and canals are the natural highways
of the country ; rivers are only utilised as a
motive power for electricity, manufactories, and
for conveying millions of logs of timber yearly
from the inland forests to the sea.   A curious
fact is that, although many parts of the interior
are far below the level of the Baltic, the latter is

gradually but surely receding from the coast, and many hitherto submerged islets off the latter have been left high and dry by the waves. You may now in places walk from one island to another on dry land, which, fifty years ago, was many fathoms under water, while signs of primitive navigation are constantly being discovered as far as twenty miles inland! It is therefore probable that the millions of islands which now fringe these shores, formed, at some remote period, one continuous strip of land. How vessels ever find their way, say from Hangö to Nystad, is a mystery to the uninitiated landsman. At a certain place there are no less than three hundred islands of various sizes crowded into an area of six square miles! Heaven preserve the man who finds himself there, in thick weather, with a skipper who does not quite know the ropes!

The provinces of which the Grand Duchy is composed are as follows, running from north to south: (1) Finnish Lapland, (2) Ostrobothnia, (3) Satakunta, (4) Tavastland, (5) Savolax, (6) Karelia, (7) Finland proper, (8) Nyland, and (9) the Åland Islands.

Finnish Lapland may be dismissed without comment, for it is a wild, barren region, sparsely populated by nomad tribes, and during the summer is practically impassable on account of its dense forests, pathless swamps, and mosquitos of unusual size and ferocity. In winter-time journeys can be made quickly and pleasantly in sledges drawn by reindeer, but at other times the country must be crossed in cranky canoes by means of a network of lakes and rivers; and the travelling is about as tough as monotony, short rations, and dirt can make it. I am told that gold has lately been discovered there, but it would need a considerable amount of the precious metal to tempt me into Finnish Lapland in summer-time.

Ostrobothnia, which lies immediately south of this undesirable district, contains the towns of Torneå and Uleåborg, but as I shall presently refer to these places at length we will pass on to the provinces of Central Finland, viz. Tavastland, Savolax, and Karelia. The Finns say that this is the heart of their country, while Helsingfors and Tammerfors constitute its brains. So crowded and complicated is the lake system in this part of Finland that water almost overwhelms dry land, and the district has been likened to one huge archipelago. Forests abound, especially in Tavastland, whence timber is exported in large quantities, while agriculture

P

flourishes in all these provinces. Crops are generally grown in the valleys, while in other parts the sides and summits of the hills are usually selected for cultivation. Large tracts of country about here once laid out for arable are now converted into grazing grounds, for the number of cattle is yearly on the increase. Dairy-farming is found to be more profitable and less risky than the raising of wheat and barley in a land where one night of frost sometimes destroys the result of a whole year's patient care and labour. The land is cleared for cultivation by felling and burning, and it is then ploughed in primitive fashion and sown, but only one harvest is generally gathered on one spot. The latter is then deserted, and the following year another patch of virgin soil takes its place. There is thus a good deal of waste, not only in land, but also in trees, which are wantonly cut down for any trifling purpose, regardless of their value or the possible scarcity in the future of timber. Accidental forest fires also work sad havoc at times, destroying thousands of pounds' worth of timber in a few hours. Pine resin burns almost as fiercely as petroleum, and it sometimes takes days to extinguish a conflagration.

Many of the poorer people in the central

provinces live solely by fishing in the lakes teeming with salmon, which find a ready market both salted and fresh. There is plenty of rough shooting to be had for the asking, but no wild animals of any size. In the far north bears are still numerous, and elk were formerly obtainable. A few of the latter still exist in the wilder parts of the country, but it is now forbidden to kill them. Some years ago the forests of Tavastland were infested with wolves, and during one fatal season a large number of cattle and even some children were devoured, but a *battue* organised by the peasantry cleared the brutes out of the country. You may now shoot hares here, and any number of wild fowl, but that is about all.

The remainder of Finland consists of Finland proper and Nyland on the south and south-western coasts, and as these comprise not only the capital, but also the large towns of Åbo and Viborg, they may be regarded as the most important, politically, commercially, and socially, in the country. Here lakes are still numerous, but insignificant in size compared with those of the interior. On the other hand, the vegetation is richer, for the oak, lime, and hazel do well, and the flora, both wild and cultivated, is much more extensive than in the central and northern districts. Several kinds of fruit are grown, and Nyland apples are famous for their flavour, while very fair pears, plums, and cherries can be bought cheaply in the markets. Currants and gooseberries are, however, sour and tasteless. In these southern districts the culture of cereals has reached a perfection unknown further north, for the farms are usually very extensive, the farmers up to date, and steam implements in general use. Dairy-farming is also carried on with excellent results and yearly increasing prosperity. Amongst the towns, Bjorneborg, Nystad, Hangö, and Kotka will in a few years rival the capital in size and commercial importance. Viborg the reader is already acquainted with, and Helsingfors will be described in the following chapter, so that it is unnecessary to say any more regarding these two leading and most important cities of Finland.

The last on the list is the Åland archipelago, which consists of one island of considerable size surrounded by innumerable smaller ones, and situated about fifty miles off the south-western coast of Finland. Here, oddly enough, Nature has been kinder than almost anywhere on the mainland, for although the greater part of the island is wild and forest-clad, the eternal pines

and silver birch trees are blended with the oak
ash, and maple, and bright blossoms such as
may and hawthorn relieve to a great extent the
monotonous green foliage of Northern Europe.

That the Ålander has much of the Swede in
his composition is shown by the neatness of his
dwellings and cleanly mode of life. He is an
amphibious creature, half mariner, half yeoman, a
sober, thrifty individual, who spends half of his
time at the plough-tail and the other at the helm.
Fishing for a kind of small herring called
"strömming" is perhaps the most important
industry, and a lucrative one, for this fish (salted)
it sent all over the country and even to Russia
proper. Farming is a comparatively recent
innovation, for the Ålanders are born men of the
sea, and were once reckoned the finest sailors in
Finland. Less than a century ago Åland har-
boured a fine fleet of sailing-ships owned by
syndicates formed amongst the peasantry, and
engaged in a profitable trade with Great Britain
and Denmark. But steamers have knocked all
this upon the head, and the commercial future of
the islands would now seem to depend chiefly
upon the fishing and agricultural industries.

The population of these Islands is under
25,000, of which the small town of Mariehamm,

the so-called capital, contains about 700 souls. Steamers touch here, so that there is no difficulty in reaching the place, which is certainly worth a visit not only for its antiquity (the Ålands were inhabited long before the mainland), but on account of the interesting ruins it contains— amongst them the Castle of Castelholm, built by Birger Jarl in the fourteenth century, and the time-worn walls of which could tell an interesting history. A part of the famous fortress of Bomarsund, destroyed by an Anglo-French fleet in 1854, may also be seen not far from Mariehamm. Plain but decent fare may be obtained here, but the fastidious will do well to avoid the smaller villages, where the Ålander's diet generally consists solely of seal-meat, salt fish, bread and milk. A delicacy eaten with gusto by these people is composed of seal-oil and the entrails of sea-birds, and is almost identical with one I saw amongst the Tchuktchis on Bering Straits. And yet the Ålanders are cleanly enough in their habits and the smallest village has its bath-house.

At one time Åland was famous for sport, and in olden days Swedish sovereigns visited the island to hunt the elk, which were then numerous. But these and most other wild animals are now

extinct and even wild fowl are scarce. Only one
animal appears to thrive : the hedgehog ; but
the natives do not appear to have discovered
its edible qualities. An English tramp could
enlighten them on this point.

The entire population of Finland amounts to
rather over two millions and a half, including a
considerable number of Swedes, who are found
chiefly in the Åland Islands, Nyland, and Finland
proper. Helsingfors, the capital, contains over
80,000 souls, and Kemi, the smallest town, near
the northern frontier, under 400. Of the other
cities, Åbo has 30,000, Tammerfors 25,000, and
Viborg 20,000 inhabitants. I should add that
there is probably no country in creation where the
population has so steadily increased, notwithstanding adverse conditions, as Finland. After the
Russian campaign of 1721 the country contained
barely 250,000 souls, and yet, although continually
harassed by war and its attendant evils, these
had increased thirty years later to 555,000.
Fifty years ago the Finns numbered a million
and a half, and the latest census shows nearly
double these figures, although in 1868 pestilence
and famine swept off over 100,000 victims.

The languages spoken in the Grand Duchy
are Finnish and Swedish, the former being used

by at least eighty-five per cent. of the population. Russian-speaking inhabitants number about 5,000, while the Lapps amount to 1,000 only, other nationalities to under 3,000. Although Swedish is largely spoken in the towns, Finnish only is heard, as a rule, in the rural districts. There is scarcely any nobility in the country, if we except titled Swedish settlers. Most Finns belong to the middle class of life, with the exception of a few families ennobled in 1809 by the Tsar of Russia on his accession as Grand Duke of Finland. The lower orders are generally quiet and reserved in their demeanour, even on festive public occasions, and make peaceable, law-abiding citizens. "'Arry" is an unknown quantity here, and "'Arriet" does not exist. A stranger will everywhere meet with studied politeness in town and country. Drive along a country road, and every peasant will raise his hat to you, not deferentially, but with the quiet dignity of an equal. The high standard of education, almost legally exacted from the lowest classes in Finland, is unusually high, for the most illiterate ploughboy may not marry the girl of his choice until he can read the Bible from end to end to the satisfaction of his pastor, and the same rule applies to the fair sex.

The climate of Finland is by no means so severe as is generally imagined. As a matter of fact, no country of a similar latitude, with the exception of Sweden, enjoys the same immunity from intense cold. This is owing to the Gulf Stream, which also imparts its genial influence to Scandinavia. In summer the heat is never excessive, the rainfall is insignificant, and thunderstorms are rare. July is the warmest, and January the coldest month, but the mean temperature of Helsingfors in mid-winter has never fallen below that of Astrakhan, on the Caspian Sea.

The weather is, however, frequently changeable, and even in summer the thermometer often rises or falls many degrees in the space of a few hours. You may sit down to dinner in the open air in Helsingfors in your shirt-sleeves, and before coffee is served be sending home for a fur coat. But this is an unusual occurrence, for a summer in Finland has been my most agreeable climatic experience in any part of the world.

The winter is unquestionably hard, and lasts about six months, from November till the middle of April. At Christmas time the sun is only visible for six hours a day. The entire surface of the country, land, lake, and river, then forms one vast and frozen surface of snow, which may be traversed by means of sledge, snowshoes, or ski. A good man on the last-named will easily cover his seven miles an hour. Although tourists generally affect this country in the open season, a true Finlander loves the winter months as much as he dislikes the summer. In his eyes boredom, heat, and mosquitos are a poor exchange for merry picnics on skis, skating contests, and sledge expeditions by starlight with pretty women and gay companions, to say nothing of the nightly balls and theatre and supper parties. Helsingfors is closed to navigation from November until June, for the sea forms an icy barrier around the coast of Finland, now no longer impenetrable, thanks to the ice-breakers at Hangö. In the north the Gulf of Bothnia is frozen for even longer.

Towards April winter shows signs of departure. By the middle of May ice and snow have almost disappeared, except in the north, where Uleåborg is, climatically, quite three weeks behind any of the southern towns. Before the beginning of June verdure and foliage have reappeared in all their luxuriance, and birds and flowers once more gladden field and forest with perfume and song. Even now an occasional shower of sleet besprinkles the land, only to melt in a few minutes, and leave it fresher and greener than before. May and June are, perhaps, the best months, for July and August are sometimes too warm to be pleasant. October and November are gloomy and depressing. Never visit Finland in the late autumn, for the weather is then generally dull and overcast, while cold, raw winds, mist and sleet, are not the exception. Midwinter and midsummer are the most favourable seasons, which offer widely different but equally favourable conditions for the comfort and amusement of the traveller.

And, if possible, choose the former, if only for one reason. No one who has ever witnessed the unearthly beauty of a summer night in Finland is likely to forget it. The Arctic Circle should, of course, be crossed to witness the midnight sun in all its glory, but I doubt if the quiet *crépuscule* (I can think of no other word) of the twilit hours of darkness is not even more weird and fascinating viewed from amid silent streets and buildings than from the sullen dreariness of an Arctic desert, which is generally (in summer) as drab and as flat as a biscuit. In Arctic Lapland, where for two months the sun never sinks below the horizon, you may read small print without difficulty throughout the night between June and August. This would be impossible in Helsingfors, where nevertheless from sunset till dawn it is never quite dark. In the far north the midnight sun affords a rather garish light; down south it sheds grey but luminous rays, so faint that they cast no shadows, but impart a weird and mysterious grace to the most commonplace surroundings. No artist has yet successfully portrayed the indescribable charm and novelty of a summer night under these conditions, and, in all probability, no artist ever will!

CHAPTER VIII

HELSINGFORS

HIS Majesty the Tsar's manifesto has not as yet (outwardly, at any rate) Russianised the capital of Finland. It will probably take centuries to do that, for Finland, like France, has an individuality which the combined Powers of Europe would be puzzled to suppress. A stranger arriving at the railway station of Helsingfors, for instance, may readily imagine himself in Germany, Austria, or even Switzerland, but certainly not within a thousand miles of Petersburg. Everything is so different, from the dapper stationmaster with gold-laced cap of German build down to the porters in clean white linen blouses, which pleasantly contrast with the malodorous sheepskins of unwashed Russia. At Helsingfors there is nothing, save the soldiery, to remind one of the proximity of Tsarland. And out in the country it is the same. The line from Mikkeli traverses a fair and prosperous district, as unlike the monotonous scenery over the border as the proverbial dock and daisy. Here are no squalid hovels and roofless sheds where half-starved cattle share the misery of their owners; no rotting crops and naked pastures; but snug homesteads, flower gardens, and neat wooden fences encircling fields of golden grain and rich green meadow land. To travel in Southern Finland after Northern Russia is like leaving the most hideous parts of the Black Country to suddenly emerge into the brightness and verdure of a sunlit Devonshire.

Had my Finnish friend at Petersburg told me that I should find at Helsingfors an hotel equal in every respect to the "Cecil" or "Savoy," I should certainly have disbelieved him. And yet, although my Finnish hostelry lacked the show and glitter of those London palaces, it was no less comfortable, and certainly much cheaper. Of course, it was the "Societetshuset," and therefore situated in the finest part of the city in full view of the harbour and principal boulevards.

Here another surprise awaited me, for the manager ushered me into a sumptuous apartment (fifteen marks a day inclusive), and retired without even asking for my passport! Nor was the latter once required from the time

I left Petersburg until I crossed the Swedish frontier. A passport, however, *may* be needed on this journey, and should therefore be taken, properly *visad*, on leaving England. Throughout European Russia it is, of course, essential. No one can enter or leave the country without it, or even even reside for a few hours in a town without its inspection by the agent of police. On arrival at Helsingfors I anticipated some trouble in this respect, for on attempting to enter a droshky to drive to the hotel a policeman politely but firmly restrained me. It was only, however, to present me with a brass disc, bearing the number of my *fiacre*—a fatherly precaution taken by the Finnish Government to protect the public against overcharge, theft, or the accidental loss of property.

Take a portion of Stockholm, with its dull but cleanly streets, enliven it with a little bit of Paris in the shape of boulevards and cafés, surround the whole with pine-clad hills and islands set in a sea of Mediterranean blue, and you have my first impression of Helsingfors, which, by the way, was founded in 1650, and now contains about 80,000 souls. The capital of Finland is, of course, small compared with Petersburg and Moscow, but it is certainly the

most pleasurable city in Northern Europe. Stockholm is perhaps finer, but lacks the lovely surroundings. Nor is it as healthy, for Helsingfors
is built upon rock, and is surrounded by breezy
fjords, forming one of the finest harbours in
Europe. A leading physician told me that since
the modern system of drainage had been introduced summer epidemics were unknown. In
winter the climate is trying, and pulmonary
diseases are prevalent owing to intense cold,
often of a damp, foggy nature.

On a bright summer's day, however, the capital
is so gay and attractive that one cannot picture
it swept by Arctic blizzards and clad in a dreary
mantle of snow; for the streets are full of life
and animation, and one need never feel bored
after dark with an excellent opera-house, two
or three theatres, and several other places of
amusement to visit. The Esplanad-Gatan is the
favourite resort—a thoroughfare formed by handsome public and private buildings and the best
hotels and shops. A beautifully kept garden
with smooth lawns and bright flower-beds runs
the length of this boulevard, which, with its
avenue of lime trees and neatly gravelled paths,
recalls bits of the Tuileries Gardens or Champs
Elysées; for there are restaurants with snowy

"ESPLANAD-GATAN," HELSINGFORS

To face page 116

dinner-tables, kiosks for toys and sweetstuff, and children with their nurses playing under the trees; only "guignol" and goat-carriages are wanting to make the illusion complete! A military band plays here twice a day in summer, but might well be spared, for the Finnish, like the Russian regimental bands, are generally execrable. A statue of Runeberg, the poet-patriot, occupies the centre of the Esplanad-Gatan, which is about half a mile long, ending at one extremity with a fine theatre and restaurant, and at the other with the quay, the market-place, and last, but not least, the "Societetshuset." By the way, the Hotel Kamp (29, Norra Esplanad-Gatan) is also an excellent house, even cheaper than the former. A wet afternoon may be pleasantly passed at the Athenæum, a handsome building presented by the State to be utilised as an academy of the fine arts. The pictures and statuary it contains would probably find favour amongst the most severe art critics in London or Paris, especially the latter, for the Finnish school has much in common with the French.

Helsingfors, so far as I could judge, is a slumless city. Although the Esplanad-Gatan is its Piccadilly and Hyde Park combined, nearly

R

all the streets are spacious, well paved, and lined with fine stone buildings of the most modern architecture. Even outlying thoroughfares are laid out with regularity, and are kept as clean and tidy as those of the most fashionable quarters. The main arteries of traffic are nearly all rectangular, and as their names are plainly shown in Finn, Swedish, and Russian, it is fairly easy to find the way about. Cab fares are by no means ruinous—fifty pennis the course, or a mark and a half the hour. Tramcars running throughout Helsingfors and its suburbs are now drawn by horses, but the latter will in a few months be replaced by electricity.

The Katerinska and Sophiska Gatans ("gatan" signifies street), which lead from the harbour to the Senate Square, are worthy of a place in the heart of any great city, while the square itself is especially interesting, for here the populace assembled on the evening already referred to of the Sunday following the manifesto. One side is occupied by the Lutheran church of St. Nicholas —a beautiful building, with lofty, star-spangled domes visible for many miles out to sea, and which affords a splendid view of Helsingfors and the surrounding country. Other sides of the square are formed by the Senate House and

University, while in the centre the imposing
statue of Alexander II. rises out of a mountain
of withered flowers and immortelles laid there
upon each anniversary of his death.   The statue
faces the University Library, with its valuable
collection of 200,000 volumes, and paintings, and
sculptures, mostly the work of Finnish artists.
It contains also a reading-room, with German
and English newspapers, which is open daily to
the public from ten till three.

Although provided with several letters of
introduction, I only found it necessary to present
one to Professor M——, a leading scientist, a
pleasant companion and admirable guide, who
spoke English fluently.   Under M——'s guidance
I visited the University, which has about a
thousand students.   The difference between the
Russian and Finnish student is as marked as
that between the *élève* of the Ecole Polytech-
nique and a Cambridge undergraduate.   In
Russia the flat cap and grey coat with silver
buttons and blue facings impart a military appearance to the mildest civilian ; but in Finland
uniforms are at a discount, and only a tiny
German cap is worn to distinguish its wearer
as a University man.   Women are admitted at
Helsingfors University, and many have graduated

in Science, Art, and Medicine.* It seemed
strange at first to see young girls walking about
in white velvet caps like those worn by the
students at Bonn and Heidelberg, but the
women of Finland have reached a stage of
emancipation as yet unknown in any other
country. They have, it is true, no political
rights, but are frequently employed in Government service, while as regards mental and even
physical employment there is very little difference
here between the sexes. Go into a bank or
railway station, and your cheque is generally
cashed or ticket handed you by a female clerk.
In the agricultural districts women work quite
as hard as men in the fields, and in the towns
are often seen sweeping the streets. Many are
even employed as stonemasons and carpenters ;
indeed, there is hardly any kind of manual labour
that a Finnish woman will not turn her hand
to, or any profession from which she is debarred,
save, perhaps, the Army and the Church. And,
in Finland at least, she generally succeeds
admirably in her business undertakings, from
the keeping of a ledger to the roofing of a

* The fees at Helsingfors University are forty marks a year
for both sexes, who study in the same classes and under the same
conditions.

house. Let me add that, notwithstanding all this independence of thought and action, the Finnish woman has never sacrificed the refinement indispensable to feminine charm and influence. Her love of home and children is as strong as that of the most domesticated German matron. One seldom meets a " Blue Stocking," as we know them, for equality of sex is an accepted fact, and there is no need for the crazy advocates of women's rights, who excite only pity and derision in England. On the other hand, the women here are certainly as well, if not better educated than those of any other European country. They are well read, musical, and artistic, generally acquainted with two or three languages, and thoroughly posted in the home and foreign topics of the day. Most of them marry at an early age, but divorce is rare, for marital infidelity is looked upon as an unpardonable crime, and punished accordingly. The man, as well as the woman, is tabooed for ever by Society. At the same time it is easier to obtain a divorce than in almost any other country. Supposing both parties agree to separate, there is no King's Proctor to prevent them. A man has only to disappear for a year, at the end of which period he is advertised for

three times in the newspapers. Should there
be no response, his wife may at once procure
her divorce and re-marry — and *vice versâ*.
Although the female considerably outnumbers
the male population of Finland, it is probably
the least immoral country in the world. The
streets of the capital after nightfall are a proof
of this, also the public places of entertainment,
any of which a lady can visit alone and unpro-
tected without fear of insult. This is strange
when we consider that Helsingfors is sandwiched
between two of the most licentious cities in
Europe—Stockholm and St. Petersburg. Vice
must, of course, exist in every large town, but
in Helsingfors the police regulations are so
cleverly framed that it is rendered as invisible,
and therefore as innocuous, as possible.

Take a walk through this fascinating city, and
you will find that pretty faces are in the majority,
mostly of the flaxen-haired, blue-eyed type. The
women, as a rule, are of the middle height, with
good figures, but are apt, like the Germans, to
become stout at an early age. "You do not see us
at our best," said M—— one afternoon, as we
strolled out to dine at the " Kapellet," a famous
open-air restaurant in the Esplanad-Gatan. "This
is summer-time, and all who can afford it send their

THE CATHEDRAL, HELSINGFORS

To face page 122

wives and daughters to the country. Come here
at Christmas, and you shall see as pretty and
well-dressed women as Paris itself can produce.
For many reasons," M—— went on, "Helsingfors
is then at its best, for from November till the spring
there is an endless round of sport and gaiety.
Sledge parties, ski contests, skating tourna-
ments, and trotting races on the ice by day, at
night-time, dancing, supper parties, music, and the
theatres." In Finland skating is a national pas-
time, although you may travel in winter throughout Russia in every direction, and never even
see a pair of skates. The Helsingfors rink is
the finest in the world, and according to M——,
when a night's fête is held, and thousands of
people meet under the stars to skate in a blaze of
electric light to exhilarating dance music, the
scene must indeed be novel and enchanting.
Trotting races are also held, and such valuable
prizes offered, that horses are sent from long
distances to compete. The Finnish record time
(over the ice) is one kilometre in one minute
forty-two seconds—truly wonderful, considering
that the fastest American trotter has never done
the same distance over a track in less than one
minute and seventeen seconds. Ice-boat sailing
is another favourite amusement amongst the

jeunesse dorée, and long trips are made at a terrific speed over the black, mirror-like ice of the larger lakes. Thus, with sport of all kinds in the daytime, and nights of Lutetian revelry, Helsingfors, during the winter season, well deserves its Finnish cognomen of "a little Paris "!

Russians in Helsingfors are rigorously excluded from social functions, or from any entertainments organised by Finlanders. It is even whispered that at a ball recently given by the Governor of Finland, General Bobrikoff, on the occasion of his daughter's birthday, that young lady was compelled to sit out the whole evening, and eventually retired in tears from the ballroom. This was, perhaps, carrying racial hatred a little too far. On the other hand, the Governor-General has only himself to thank for his almost universal unpopularity, for a month rarely passes without the issue of some vexatious decree from the Government House at Helsingfors. Some weeks ago a circular note was issued requesting that all official communications should be worded in Russian, the first step towards the elimination of the Finnish language. The Governor then turned his attention to the postage of Finland. This must be abolished, and replaced by the ordinary

Russian stamps. This measure was enforced on the 15th of August, 1900, but not until important meetings had been held in Helsingfors and other large towns to protest against this latest infringement on the rights of the Grand Duchy. The postage question excited special indignation throughout Finland. Hostile demonstrations took place in the capital, and a revolutionary stamp was struck at the expense of the leading merchants, and distributed in its millions amongst the people. The stamp, which is pasted *inside* the envelope, bears the Lion of Finland in yellow, with the word "Suomi" above it, and the word "Finland" below, in white letters. The black ground is emblematical of the mourning into which the country has been plunged by the gradual extermination of her rights and liberty. The use of these contraband stamps is, of course, strictly forbidden, and I read at Helsingfors a street placard stating that persons found with them would be very severely punished.

His Imperial Majesty the Tsar appears to be as esteemed and respected in the capital and elsewhere as the Governor-General is the reverse. Throughout my travels in Finland I never once heard a disparaging remark anent Nicholas II., which circumstance, in view of the reports that occasionally reach England, may strike the reader as curious, but which is nevertheless a fact. Wherever I went there was far less enmity shown by all classes towards the head of the State than to its local governing body. Thus I was even told a pretty little anecdote relating to the late Alexander III. by a prominent Finnish patriot in Helsingfors which may bear repetition.

His Majesty was upon one occasion fishing in the vicinity of Viborg incognito, and attended only by an aide-de-camp. Sport had been bad all the morning until an old woodcutter passed by and suggested another kind of bait—a species of worm peculiar to the district. In less than an hour several fine fish had been landed by the Emperor, who was so pleased at his success that he ordered an adjournment, to the dwelling of the peasant whose advice had proved so useful, for lunch. Here the trout were cooked and partaken of, the woodcutter's daughter waiting upon the Imperial guest, who was struck by her tearful eyes and downcast appearance.

"Why is she so sad?" inquired the Tsar of her father at the close of the repast.

"Her *fiancé* is going away to-morrow to

serve in the Army. They cannot marry, poor souls! Our Grand Duke takes them away for too long."

" But he takes so few of them!" said the Emperor amusedly. " Where is he, this *fiancé* ?"

" In the next house."

" Go and fetch him !"

A good-looking lad presently entered and nervously eyed the stalwart, flaxen-bearded figure before him.

" So you want to marry your pretty little neighbour ?"

A shy nod was the reply.

" Well, give her a kiss, and tell her you are not going away. General, write this man a dispensation from military service!"

And the Emperor rose to leave the place.

" Great heavens! can it be possible? Who are you ?" cried the amazed woodcutter, throwing up his arms. " Why, the Tsar himself could scarcely——!"

" I *am* the Tsar!" said Alexander III., turning back from the threshold. " The Tsar of all the Russias in Saint Petersburg! At Viborg I am only Grand Duke of Finland."

Our dinner over at the unconventional hour

of 5 p.m., the Professor and I lighted our cigars and strolled past the quays, with their busy wharves and shipping, to the Brunnsparken—beautifully laid out public gardens overlooking, on the one hand, the city and harbour, and on the other a blue plain of sea. In summer this is as favourite a resort as the Esplanad-Gatan, for here the jaded city man can eat his dinner at an excellent restaurant while enjoying the cool breezes from the Baltic. On the summit of a grassy slope hard by is a handsome observatory founded by the Finnish scientist Nervander in 1843, which was at that period considered one of the finest astronomical establishments in Europe. From this point Helsingfors is seen at its best, the golden dome of the cathedral towering over a mass of spires, fire towers, and white buildings, set off by greenery ; the quays alive with the bustle of locomotives and steam cranes, and the busy harbour crowded with craft of all kinds, from the grimy whaler to the white-sailed pleasure yacht. I can plainly distinguish my open window at the " Societetshuset," and beneath it the market-place, a bright patch of colour, with its gaily coloured booths, fruit, and flowers ; while inland, beyond a confused mass of masonry and verdure, the picture is framed in pine forest, studded at intervals with shining lakes, for all the world like bits of crystal sunk into a piece of dark enamel.

Then back again for a saunter through the streets to while away the time until an evening at the theatre shall end the day. The shops of Helsingfors are quite equal to those of any European capital, and you may purchase any-thing, from a suit of Scotch tweeds to a box of Parisian bonbons, at a more than reason-able price, considering the distance and duty. The scarcity of Russian goods exposed for sale was surprising. Even in the best library on the Esplanad-Gatan, where the latest French, English, and German works were procurable, there was a marked absence of Russian litera-ture. Another hint may be useful to travellers. Wishing to purchase an American remedy for neuralgia, I entered a palatial pharmacy, but found that here (as in Russia) the sale of the most harmless drug bearing a duty stamp is prohibited. Even a grain of calomel cannot be obtained without the special permission of a medical man. It is well, therefore, to take any patent medicine that may be required out from England.

We found the Swedish theatre, a prettily

s

decorated house, crowded to the utmost, for M—— told me that the piece was a very popular one. Being unacquainted with the language, the name upon the play bill told me nothing—the players less; and it was some time before I realised that my old friend *The Private Secretary* was as usual delighting its audience. A translation of *The Manxman*, by Hall Caine, was to be produced on the following evening, and M—— told me that many English plays see the light here very shortly, as a rule, after their production in England. Modern English and American literature would also seem to be popular, for I frequently came across translations of the works of Rudyard Kipling, Anthony Hope, and Mark Twain, which (I was told) have a large and ready sale even in the smallest towns of the interior.

CHAPTER IX

HELSINGFORS

"WHAT a glorious day!" said the Professor, with a glance at the sunlit harbour while draining a crystal flagon of Pilsener. "Why should we not make a little excursion by steamer to Sveaborg?"

It was barely ten o'clock a.m., and we had just partaken of a meal consisting of soup, grilled salmon, and beefsteak washed down by beverages, which, in England, are generally consumed after midday. But this is called "lunch" in Finland; and, after all, custom is everything! Fortunately the *chef de cuisine* at the "Societetshuset" was an artist, and I therefore suffered no ill effects.

"No, I will tell you what," added my guest, as if struck by a sudden inspiration, "Hangö is a place you ought to see. We will go to Hangö." To Hangö indeed! It was precisely as though a friend in London had suggested a little dinner at Richmond and abruptly abandoned it in favour of a trip to York! For Hangö, although only one hundred and twenty miles from Helsingfors as the crow flies, is a journey of over six hours by rail. But the Finlander resembles the Russian at least in one

THE PROFESSOR

respect : he has the vaguest ideas of time and distance. The virility of aged people in both these countries is remarkable. Here, for instance, was this portly Professor, a man well on in the sixties, eager to embark on a long and fatiguing journey at a moment's notice (and without luggage) with all the exuberance of a boy of sixteen; and I have met Siberian octogenarians who thought nothing of three or four days in a sleigh, in an Arctic temperature, with nothing to subsist upon but some gritty black bread and a few glasses of tea.

Hangö is the most southern town in Finland. As it is a small, very modern watering-place, barely thirty years old, with nothing of local interest save a mammoth hotel and bathing establishments, I was unwilling to travel so far to see so little. In winter Hangö is worth a visit if only to witness the working of the " Murtaja," a powerful ice-breaker, which maintains steamship communication with Sweden throughout the year; but in summer there is literally nothing to do but to stroll about a commonplace casino and watch the bathers. " One can do that any day at Brighton or Dieppe," I remarked, "and perhaps less expensively," for the high charges of this tiny Finnish watering-place are notorious. But M——— was as keen on the excursion as any cheap tripper, urging as an inducement that the place was visited by the English fleet during the Crimean War, when its forts, being untenable, were destroyed by the Russians. The granite of Hangö, too, was

T

the finest in the world. "But if the forts had disappeared," I argued, "why go ? And as for the granite—well, I had seen that at Petersburg !" So the Professor resignedly ordered another bock ; and Sveaborg was finally settled upon.

A summer's day at Helsingfors need never be tedious, for numerous excursions may be made to the various islands at sea or lakes a short distance away. Every point of attraction has its hotel or café, so that it is never necessary to take provisions. Amongst the islands the most popular resort is Hogholm, a lovely spot, with park-like scenery and pretty gardens encircling a restaurant, with glorious views over land and sea. Finlanders, like the French, live largely in the open air, and here on a fine summer's evening you may see hundreds of people dining at little tables under the trees, to the strains of a string band. Hogholm is easily reached in a few minutes by a small steamer which leaves a landing-place near the "Societetshuset" every half-hour. Thurholm, Stansvik, and Willings are all bright and pleasant little places with picturesque scenery and pure air, but it is well to visit them on a week-day, and the same may be said of Hogholm. For on Sundays thousands of workmen come here with their wives and children, and the place becomes a kind of Rosherville on a happy day, without, however, the repellent revelry that is the usual accompaniment of a day out with English " 'Arry." Here you may see the people cooking their dinners at queer little fireplaces in the ground provided for the purpose and eating it *al fresco*, and for those who do not object to a crowd the sight is a pretty and interesting one. Further afield, Borgä may be reached by land as well as by water, and is well worth seeing, for this quaint old city dates from the thirteenth century, and its cathedral is one of the most perfect specimens existing of mediæval Finnish architecture. It was from this building that Alexander I. of Russia issued his famous proclamation in 1809. The great Finnish poet Runeberg lived in Borgä for many years, and his house, which at his death was purchased by the State, is still shown exactly as it appeared during his lifetime. If the interior has really been preserved intact, Runeberg must have been, as regards furniture, of a singularly inartistic turn of mind. But perhaps the patriot was too deeply engrossed in literary work to be mindful of earthly surroundings. The sea route to Borgä from Helsingfors is one of the pleasantest runs down the coast, but, in any case, a whole day must be devoted to this excursion. All the places I have mentioned can be visited at a trifling cost. The excursion to Borgä and back, for instance, including dinner and railway or steamboat fare, can be made luxuriously for under fifteen marks!

No stranger is allowed to visit the fortress of Sveaborg without a special permit from the military authorities, and there are so many formalities to be gone through respecting passports, identity, etc., that to obtain one is generally a question of days. With the well-known and popular Professor as a companion, however, it was merely a matter of minutes. In less than an hour after lunch we were scudding across the breezy harbour towards our destination in a noisy little steamer crowded with grey-coated, gold-laced Russian officers—bonâ fide Russians these, for the defence of this Gibraltar of the North is (for obvious reasons) not entrusted to the Finns. A spy would stand a poor chance at Sveaborg, for from the moment of landing we were surrounded by half a dozen lynx-eyed guards, who watched our every movement and who only left us when we re-embarked. And even with all these precautions one is only permitted to examine the least important works.

So far as one can judge, Sveaborg is as impregnable as our Mediterranean stronghold. Even in 1855 the allied French and English fleets bombarded it with little effect, and since those days the place has been greatly strengthened. The fortress, or rather forts, are built on a succession of islands, seven in number, which are situated about four miles south-west of Helsingfors. The original works were commenced in 1749 by Count Ehrensvard, High Admiral of Sweden (who is interred upon Vargo, the principal islet of the group), and its garrison now consists of 5,000 men (on a peace footing) and nearly 1,000 guns of heavy calibre and the most modern construction. Once only has Sveaborg fallen, when, in the year 1808, it was ceded to Russia by its Swedish commandant, Admiral Cronstedt, under circumstances as suspicious as those that surrounded the surrender of Metz by General Bazaine. Cronstedt is, rightly or wrongly, supposed to have been bribed by the enemy—at any rate, the fact remains that he hauled down his colours and surrendered with 6,000 men and two ships of the line without firing a shot. I was told that Sveaborg is provisioned to sustain a siege of five years with a garrison of 5,000 men, and could certainly hold out for that period against the continued attack of the two first-class Powers, but as my informant, a loquacious sergeant who took us round, had already related several fairy tales regarding the defences of Vladivostok (with which I am acquainted), I am inclined to doubt this statement. On the other hand, the fortress of Sveaborg would undoubtedly be a very hard nut for any nation to crack. The sergeant had served in the East, and was therefore not imbued with an affection for England. He gleefully told us that some time ago an English tourist who had landed with a camera was kept in durance vile for two days in a casement. " More for the fun of the thing than anything else," he added, " for no one thought the poor man was really dangerous." Take not, therefore, a kodak• to Sveaborg!

To thoroughly visit Sveaborg takes several hours, and we only steamed away from the place at dusk. " We will sup at the Yacht Club," said the ever-active Professor, adding, " There it is," as we rounded the entrance to the harbour, and pointing to a picturesque islet. I had frequently noticed the place from the hotel, without realising that the handsome building with lawns and gardens sloping to the water was the headquarters of the Nyland Yacht Club.

A fleet of trim and light-sparred vessels anchored off it might have told me as much ; but I was not even aware that Helsingfors possessed a yacht club, much less that it consisted of four hundred members, many of whom own racing craft built in the best English yards. A large sum of money is given away yearly in prizes, which have lately been sailed for by French and English yachts. The club-house resembled an English country house, with its homely-looking rooms and cosy furniture. By the way, a culinary novelty was here revealed to me in the shape of the " flundra," a salt-water fish, which I may commend to the reader's notice. It is something between a sole and a sterlet, and is of a delicate and delicious flavour. I also tasted another fish in Helsingfors, the " bräcke," which should not be overlooked, but to be appreciated by an epicure " bräcke " should be broiled by a native artist.

While returning to shore in the darkness our little steam launch narrowly escaped collision with a large liner, ablaze with lights, which was making for the quay. A torrent of abuse in real Billingsgate from the steamer's bows proclaimed her nationality, but the Professor only smiled, " Our best customers," he said placidly. " Most

of our trade is done with England." This was
the third vessel of considerable size that I had
seen either entering or leaving port during my
short stay, and I mentioned the fact. "Yes,"
said M——, "our trade is every year increasing
to an incredible extent. Minerals, grain, paper
pulp, tar, cattle, and even horses are now
among our exports, to say nothing of frozen
meat. Nickel, now so valuable, has lately been
discovered in the north. What are the imports?
Well, chiefly woven goods, cotton, coffee, tea,
sugar, wine, and tobacco."

"It is curious," I said, "one hears all about
Russian trade in England, but the commerce of
Finland is very rarely mentioned."

"My friend, a good bell is heard afar," said
M—— sententiously,—" but a bad one is heard
still further!"

"But has not grain occasionally to be imported
into Finland?" deeming it wise to change the
conversation.

"Only in very unfavourable years. Occasionally, especially in the north, one night's frost will
destroy the crops throughout a whole district.
Large quantities of rye, barley, etc., are then
imported from Russia, for as yet it is only in
the south of Finland that modern methods of

agriculture prevail, and most of the implements come from England. In the north the shovel and hoe have not as yet been superseded."

"Then agriculture is the chief occupation of the peasantry ?"

"By no means. It used to be, but cattle-breeding has of late years been found so successful that dairy-farming runs it very close. Our natural meadows, good pasturage, and abundance of water render Finland an idyllic grazing ground. 'Be a cow,' says an old Finnish proverb, 'and you will be well taken care of, as a horse you will stand no chance!' But this is now hardly correct, for the Government gives premiums for improvement in the breed of horses as well as cattle."

"I presume, with all this increase of foreign trade, your shipping has considerably increased ?"

"Why certainly," replied the Professor; "especially as regards steam navigation. In 1878 Finland could only boast of under ten thousand steamships. She has now nearly forty thousand. Twenty years ago the port of Helsingfors only possessed about fifty vessels all told, and nearly half of those sailing-ships. Now we have several steamship companies, the largest of which —The Finland Steamship Company—has alone

a fleet of thirty-five steamers, with a large carrying capacity and excellent accommodation for
passengers. That was one of their ships we
passed just now at such uncomfortably close
quarters. Sailing-vessels are fast dying out, even
in the north, except for fishing purposes."

"And railways?" I asked, as we landed and
strolled up the quay, now brilliant with electric
light. "Have they also gone ahead as satis-
factorily as your mercantile navy?"

"In another ten years, my dear sir, there will
be very few places in Finland not attainable by
rail. Everything, however, depends upon the
Emperor, who can scarcely have foreseen the
effect his manifesto would have upon our emigration returns. In 1898, for instance, only thirty
thousand Finns left the country, but last year*
forty-six thousand steady, hard-working citizens
sailed for America, which, out of a population
of only two and a half millions, is, to say
the least of it, disquieting! As to railways, we
have already six hundred miles of them actually
under operation, and other lines are in course
of construction. One is even projected some
distance into Lapland, where gold has lately
been found to exist in paying quantities. It

* 1899.

has been worked there by the natives in a primitive manner for many years."

We had now reached the hotel, and being rather weary, I declined the genial Professor's invitation to accompany him to a smoking-concert given in his honour by some favourite pupils. Truly a wonderful old gentleman, I thought, as I watched him striding away up the street with the buoyancy of a man half his age. No wonder this plucky little land has gone ahead, with men of that stamp for its backbone!

A week may well be passed in Helsingfors, for there is plenty to see and to do; and, thanks to my good friend the Professor, I was able to carry away delightful recollections of my visit. A stranger unacquainted with the language is lost here without a guide, and the paid article is not yet procurable at the hotels. Nor have the agencies of the ubiquitous Cook yet reached Finland, or even Russia. There is, however, a "Finnish Tourist Association," which undertakes to supply information of all kinds. A ticket of "membership" costs only three marks, and is well worth the money, for it entitles the holder to a reduction of prices on board many of the steamers and at several hotels, while it enables him to obtain useful and reliable information regarding sport and travel in the interior. The offices of this association are open throughout the summer season at No. 15, Norra Esplanad-Gatan, Helsingfors, and the visitor travelling inland should not fail to pay them a visit. I may add, for the benefit of fishermen, that English rods and tackle of all kinds are to be found at " Lindebäck's Sporting Magazin," 30, Unions-Gatan, where the sportsman can also obtain valuable hints as to the best shooting and fishing to be obtained throughout the country.

CHAPTER X

A RAINY DAY

"DRIP, drip," went the rain from the roof, sleet rattled sharply against the window panes, and, far out at sea, a steam syren moaned faintly. I arose from a comfortable bed to look upon a grey and sodden world bemantled in mist. Towards midday I left the capital in a cheerless drizzle by a train that crawled through driving showers to the ancient town of Tavastehus, an attractive place, perhaps, in sunshine, but, as I saw it, the picture, under a leaden sky, of washed-out desolation. At the railway station the good Professor had already laden my carriage - rack with newspapers, blandly oblivious of the fact that I could not read a word of his language. The journals were, however, interesting, if only to show the marvellous progress made in this direction within the past few years. In 1846 there were only two newspapers in the

U   145

country, published weekly at its northern and southern extremities, Åbo and Uleåborg. But about this period Johann Snelman, the father of Finnish journalism, published his paper, *The Saima*, at Kuopio, and notwithstanding the restrictions imposed by the Russian Censure, managed to form the nucleus of the now important Finnish Press. In Petersburg Snelman's venture was viewed with suspicion, and, in 1850, the persecutions of the Censure reached a climax by the issue of an order that "nothing must be published in Finland but matters pertaining to the Church and domestic economy," subjects hardly calculated to raise a circulation by leaps and bounds. But this occurred before the Crimean War, at the close of which a brighter era dawned for Finnish journalism. In 1862 the first daily paper, the *Helsingfors Dagblad*, appeared, and with such success that it was soon followed by the publication of other daily journals in the provinces. At the present day there is hardly a town of any importance without its newspaper, while Åbo and Helsingfors can each boast of at least half a dozen, in the Finnish and Swedish languages, to suit all tastes. The weirdly named *Hubvudstadbladet* is the *Times* of Helsingfors, which city has also its Finnish

Daily Telegraph and *Graphic*, to say nothing of two well-illustrated and smartly written comic papers, the *Strix* and *Sondags-Nisse*, which are quite equal to any French or German publications of the kind. In 1897 sixty newspapers (including

A LITTLE NEWS

eleven " dailies ") were published in thirty Finnish towns, a pretty good average for such a young and sparsely populated country. Some of these journals are of enormous size, of nearly twice the dimensions of, say, the London *Standard*, for advertisement yearly grows more popular.

Monthly reviews and magazines are also published in the capital, excellent productions, dealing with all kinds of subjects ; science, art, agriculture, sport, and even photography—all these have special periodicals of their own. But the Censor, that bugbear of the Russian journalist, is ever threatening, like a black cloud, to blot out the sunlight of literary progress. Scarcely a week passes without interference in some shape or another, although the moderate tone of the Finnish Press regarding politics should entitle it to licence and liberty even in the most despotic land. Nevertheless, the life of a Finnish journalist is not a happy one. The more honour to those who possess the courage and patience to persevere under, often, apparently hopeless conditions.

It was all through the Professor that I stayed at Tavastehus. "You will like the place very much," were my friend's parting words, but a few hours later I recalled his genial personality with anything but amiable feelings. The journey, one of three hours, would probably be accomplished in England in one-third of the time. On the other hand, I would cheerfully have prolonged it far into the night, and thus have escaped a day of unutterable boredom, for the cosy railway carriage was far more comfortable than the dreary hostelry I found at my journey's end. There is no first class on the lines north of Helsingfors, but the second-class carriages (on the corridor system) are luxurious—in fact, all the arrangements for the comfort and convenience of travellers are excellent. Luggage, for instance, is quickly and securely registered, without any of the fuss or bother which on the Continent generally entails arrival at a station an hour before the train starts. The officials are generally obliging, and always honest. On leaving Helsingfors I was pursued by a porter to whom I had given a mark, and who, being under the impression that I had made a mistake, wished to return it.

My carriage was shared by a Finnish farmer and his wife, who spoke English and who (after they had run through the usual catechism) proved agreeable companions, although I could have dispensed with a baby who had just been vaccinated, and who frequently and loudly proclaimed the fact. Papa informed me that he was an " anti-Jennerite," but that in Finland vaccination is compulsory, any infringement of the law being severely punished. He was returning to his large dairy farm near Tammerfors, which (after the manner

x

of hospitable Finns) he invited me to inspect, and
I afterwards did so.   Also, like most Finns, papa
was a confirmed grumbler.   His country was
going to the dogs ; nothing was rightly managed ;
and, above all, the taxes were abominably high.
This I could scarcely believe, having ascertained
that the greater part of the revenue of Finland
is derived from the Customs and woods and
forests pertaining to the Government.   My fellow-
traveller seemed astonished to hear that Finns
pay the lightest taxes of any country in Europe,
but statistics prove the fact.   The heaviest is the
Income-Tax, paid by all with a yearly income
of over £32.   This varies in different towns and
districts, but the average amount levied is about
three per cent.   There is also a Church-Tax
of half a mark per cent., and lastly a Poll-Tax
on every householder of two marks for each male,
and one mark for each female living under his
roof.   Farmers pay a Land-Tax, which is, however, very insignificant.   Thus a man with, say,
£500 a year is only mulcted of about £18 in all to
maintain his country.   Would that we could say
the same in England !

I have mentioned in a preceding chapter that,
at this season of the year, it seldom rains in
Finland.   I should perhaps have added that when

it does a heavy and protracted fall generally
atones for weeks of drought! The cabs of
Tavastehus are ill-adapted for wet weather, and
my miserable droshki splashed and floundered
along the miry streets, which occasionally resembled shallow rivers slowly rising under the
pitiless downpour. My travelling companions
had urged me to accompany them on to Tammer-

A PLACE TO AVOID

fors, adding that under the circumstances Tavastehus was distinctly a place to avoid. And
I entered the gloomy portals of mine inn quite
of their opinion—the more so that in the hurry
of departure my waterproof coat had been left
at Helsingfors, and I was now drenched to the
skin. "No, no; I will telephone," said the
landlord, when I suggested the despatch of a wire

for the needful "aquascutum." "Telephone to
Helsingfors?" I asked, with some surprise.
"Throughout Finland if you like," was the
smiling reply. "To Uleåborg itself! We have
over three hundred stations in the country, and
all the towns (and a good many villages) have
telephonic communication with the capital." And
my host hurried away to the office as though
he were announcing the most ordinary fact in the
world. The cost of telegams here is reasonable
enough. Messages for Finland are sent for fifty
pennis and ten additional pennis per word, while
a cablegram to New York costs under four marks
a word.

A Siberian post-house excepted, I know of no
place in the world so depressing as a Finnish
hotel in bad weather. Helsingfors is an exception, for there are covered ways and galleries
which, although not so gay as the arcades of the
"Palais Royal," are certainly not so gloomy as
the Westminster Aquarium. There are no stage
performances or diving maidens, it is true, but
you have cafés, shops, with an occasional picture
gallery or waxwork show, where one may pass
the afternoon in comparative comfort and kill
time—out of the wet. Tavastehus, however, had
no such comforts for the weary wayfarer, for it is

a primitive little place of only five thousand souls, with the irregular, patchy appearance of most towns frequently destroyed by fire. In 1831 it was razed to the ground by a conflagration in which many perished, and there have been one or two large fires since. As for amusements, I could not even look forward to a fifth-rate theatre in the evening. "Was there anything to see in fine weather?" I asked of a seedy-looking hall porter, and a list of local attractions a yard long was unrolled for my benefit. "Plenty to see—to-day, if I liked. There was the park (such a beautiful park!) and Gustavus III.'s church, several breweries, and the Castle of Krönborg, built in the thirteenth century by Birger Jarl, but now converted into a female penitentiary!" Finland is noted for its model penal system, and, as delegate to the Paris Prison Congress of 1895, I was enabled to realise the admirable administration of even its smallest gaols. But there was no need, to-day, to increase the gloom of my surroundings by the sight of fellow-creatures in captivity. Hanwell would have been a suitable residence for anyone setting out on such an afternoon for a damp, chilly church or distant park—however beautiful or picturesque. "Was there a billiard-room?"

" No." " A reading-room ?" " No." In short,
there was nothing to do but to consume innumerable cigarettes in a dingy little restaurant while
a waiter peacefully snored in a corner, and
study the gaudy advertisements of someone's
gout pills, or somebody else's beer, which
alone embellished the grimy walls. They were
gaudy, crude productions, for Finland is young
in the art of advertisement. Wearying of
this occupation and a nasal concert, I retired
to my sleeping-apartment, which was cheerless
enough, but a glance through its fly-blown
windows revealed a still worse aspect. At
my feet a storm-bedraggled garden bereft of
colour, surrounded by drenched and drooping
limes, through the foliage of which the wind
moaned fitfully ; opposite a row of melancholy
houses with miniature cascades pouring from
their gleaming roofs ; in the street an occasional
droshki galloping madly, axle deep in mire, to
gain shelter ; and no other sign of human life but
the inevitable policeman crouching in oilskins
under a doorway. At intervals a sharp gust
of wind would drive the rain before it in a dense
cloud, and shake the old inn to its foundations, to
die away again into silence broken only by the
ceaseless murmur of falling rain and the dripping

TAVASTEHUS

To face page 154

from the eaves. I looked at the sky; it was lifeless, spongy, and grey. At the earth; it was much the same; and hopeless depression was the natural result.

"Il pleure dans mon cœur,
Comme il pleut dans la ville!"

wrote Verlaine, and I could almost realise, at Tavastehus, the feelings of the great French poet when he penned the lines. As for the Professor, I regret to own that I more than once mentally consigned him to a considerably warmer climate than that of Aden in August!

When night closed in the wind had risen to a gale, with blizzards of blinding sleet. The evening was damp and cold, and I was not sorry to find a good fire blazing in the restaurant, furnished with an English fireplace in place of the usual stuffy Russian stove. Lights and closely drawn curtains now lent an air of cheerfulness to the dark and comfortless "salle-à-manger" of the afternoon. The storm had kept the good folk of Tavastehus indoors, and only one guest was in the restaurant. His sociability was evinced by an invitation in English to share a table by the fireplace. "Sit right here!" cried the stranger in accents that unmistakably hailed from across the Herring-pond; "it ain't anyways too warm to-night!"

The speaker was one of those deplorable beings, an Americanised German Jew. I thought as much, for his name recalled Rhine vintages; while, if a Christian, he could certainly have recovered heavy damages (in any French law court) against his nose. At first I held aloof, for the Teutonic Israelite combined with the Yankee twang and aggressive manners acquired in the New World is not a desirable personality. Having met the species on both sides of the Atlantic, I speak from experience. But after this solitary, miserable day I would cheerfully have hobnobbed with a Tchuktchi, and therefore took a seat opposite the Hebrew. He was not prepossessing. Indeed, a lonely road on a dark night would have rendered his society distinctly obnoxious. And yet there was a certain frankness about the man that disarmed the distrust engendered by shabby garments and a shifty eye. My companion expanded over coffee and liqueurs (which, by the way, I was left to pay for), and became still more confidential over a bowl of punch which he was good enough to propose and concoct also at my expense. But the poor devil's pockets were evidently not too well lined, although, according to his own account, he had just returned from a prosperous tour in America. "Yes, *sir*," cried my new acquaintance, ladling out a second jorum of liberal proportions. "I guess I've made my pile this time!" and I thought he might have expended a little more of it upon his wardrobe.

My friend had, it appeared, left his birthplace, Hamburg, with his parents at an early age to reside in Russia, which country his family had abandoned to settle in Helsingfors. Being adventurously inclined, he had emigrated to America, for, according to his account, the administration of Finland is quite as intolerant where Jews are concerned as Russia itself. I doubted this at the time, also whether the genial beverage of which my friend was freely partaking was not responsible for some exaggeration where the wrongs of his people were concerned. But subsequent inquiry proved the accuracy of his statements, and a proof that drastic measures are taken to keep them out of the country is shown by the fact that there are very few Jews in Finland. Those there are live chiefly in Åbo and Helsingfors, and are mostly the families of men who have served in the Army, and who upon their discharge have been per-

mitted to settle in the country. Even then every
effort is made to remove them by the framing of
special laws and social taboo, and this although
they are generally harmless, law-abiding citizens,
generally employed as tailors and dealers in old
clothes. On the other hand, Jews pay the same
taxes as the Finns, and enjoy to a great extent
the same privileges, with one important exception: they may not marry even amongst themselves while residing in the country. Moreover,
a Jew who has married abroad is perpetually
banished from the country, and may never return
to the home he has left.

Under these circumstances my loquacious
friend was naturally not inclined in favour of the
Finns, especially as towards midnight his liba-
tions impelled him to inform me that the lady
of his choice had declined to forsake her Fatherland, notwithstanding the impassioned entreaties
which my friend was now on his way to
Bjorneborg to renew. "Can you imagine such
heartlessness?" cried the Jew, with a moistening
eye, which the punch was perhaps partly account-
able for; "but there is no good to be got out of
this country and its beastly people! The Finns
talk of their fine towns and railways, of their
riches and commercial enterprise. Where are

they? Why, sir, I guess the smallest city in
Texas would knock spots out of Helsingfors;
and then their business men. Where is the one
who can make what I call a pile, and having
made it, can keep it out of the clutches of those

"NOSSIR"

savages across the border? Look at this hotel—
not fit for a dog to lie in, and not a cocktail to be
got in the place! Bah! The very thought of
this one-horse country makes me sick!" and
my friend once more seized the punch ladle
with an energy that made me thankful that his

previous search for stimulants had been unsuccessful. " Nossir !" cried the Israelite, upon
whom the hot jorums were rapidly taking effect,
as we parted for the night. " So long as Russia
bosses this country, I guess you will never find
me investing much capital in Finnish concerns !"
—which, indeed, I could well believe, seeing that
the speaker's available wealth apparently consisted of a rusty black suit, a brown paper parcel,
and a diamond ring suspiciously suggestive of
Christmas crackers.

CHAPTER XI

TAMMERFORS·

I LEFT Tavastehus by an early train the following day, and did not see my Semitic friend again. Perhaps he had

> " Awakened in the morning
> With a feeling in his head
> Suggestive of mild excesses
> Before he retired to bed " !

—for his method of brewing whisky punch was original, and left very little room for hot water.

Tammerfors is called the " Manchester of Finland," but bears, outwardly, no resemblance whatever to the English Cottonopolis. For there are no brick warehouses, black streets, and towering chimneys, none of the grime and smoke that usually befoul a commercial city. Tammerfors, in short, is one of the prettiest towns in Finland, and you may search in vain for any visible signs of the labour and industry that have brought the place to its

Y   161

present condition of wealth and prosperity. As the train neared the township I could scarcely believe that its handsome white buildings, esplanades, and gardens were a centre of mercantile activity. At first sight Tammerfors is more like a pleasure resort than a business town.

A glorious day had succeeded one of damp and misery, and the country through which we journeyed for about a couple of hours from Tavastehus looked deliciously fresh and green after the rain, although the hay crop had evidently suffered. The latter is not gathered as in England, but is dried on long poles stuck into the ground with crossbars at intervals to stack the grass upon; a practical method, for in wet seasons the hay is clear of the damp earth, and being ventilated by a constant current of air, dries very rapidly. Less labour, too, is needed than when it has to be turned and raked in the sun. Most of the land about here is carefully drained, which accounts for its fertile appearance, while the fields were inclosed by the neat wooden palisades that in Finland form an excellent substitute for hedges. Two uprights some eight feet high are placed about eight inches apart at short intervals. These are connected by two horizontal poles five to six

TAMMERFORS

To face page 162

feet from the ground, between which sticks are laid slanting, forming a strong and durable fence.

I found the railway stations on this line even superior to those west of Helsingfors. Nearly all possessed a clean, well-managed restaurant, opening on to gardens with seats and summer-houses alongside the platform, reminding one of Switzerland or the Tyrol without the unpleasant overcrowding of those tourist-ridden lands. Indeed, were it not for the grim hand of supremacy that is slowly closing on this sunny land and its lovable people, Finland would be an idyllic country to live in. To-day, for instance, at Torjala, nearing Tammerfors, I noticed that the name of the station, although freshly painted, was being erased. It appeared, as usual, in two languages, Finnish and Russian, in the order named, but, according to an edict just issued from Helsingfors, Russia was, in future, to figure first upon the board.

The journey from Tavastehus to Tammerfors may also be accomplished by steamer *via* the Rapids of Valkiakoski (where there are some large paper mills) and Kejsarasen, so lovely a spot that the natives aver that the Saviour was here tempted by Satan, and beheld the earth in its most entrancing beauty. But there is a tiresome drive and railway interval before Tammerfors is reached, and I therefore chose the direct route by rail.

I have said that on my arrival the cleanliness of Tammerfors for a manufacturing town surprised me, but the mystery was explained when I found that coal and wood are scarcely ever used here. Water is the cheap and simple element that enables the Finnish manufacturer to read of coal strikes with composure, and shrug his shoulders at the price of fuel. But although the force and volume capable of turning any number of mills is generally at his door, the favourable position of Tammerfors is, in this respect, unequalled throughout the country. For it stands on the banks of a river that is almost a rapid in itself, and which unites the two enormous lakes of Nasijarvi and Pyhajarvi. Thus the overwhelming torrent which rushes through the very centre of the town supplies, almost free of cost, a motive power that, in England, would entail an enormous yearly expenditure. Some time ago an English scientist discovered that if we could make use of all the rain that falls in the United Kingdom it would give us in twelve months over six million horsepower. Finland, with her thousands of lakes, rapids, and rivers, could therefore attain prodigious results from the same natural source—but this is a problem for Mr. Holt Schooling, and not for me!

The first thing that strikes a stranger in Tammerfors is the amazing number of bicycles. In Helsingfors almost every fourth inhabitant cycles, but here the percentage must be even greater. During the short walk to my hotel from the railway station I was, more than once, nearly annihilated at the crossings. When the automobile craze reaches here, I shudder to think of the results. Meanwhile, everyone uses the wheel—men, women, and children—even babies who should be in arms instead of mounted on a "byke." Most of the latter were of British or American make, but a few of local production were neatly turned out. A tax of four marks must be paid by the owner on every machine, which must also bear a registration number in case of accidents, and the latter, judging from the reckless riding I saw, must be pretty frequent. The roads in Finland are mostly hard, level, and well adapted for cycling, and in summer-time a pleasant tour could be made in this manner throughout the country. No freight is paid on

z

bicycles on the lake steamers, and the railway charges are moderate.

After the gloomy (not to say dirty) hostelry at Tavastehus, I was prepared to find dubious board and lodging here. It was therefore an agreeable surprise to find that the "Societet-shuset" was, although a one-storied wooden building, quite equal in every respect to the Helsingfors hotel, indeed, the apartments were even more luxurious. One does not expect to find bedrooms with brass beds, cheerful chintz curtains, and white furniture (à *la* Maple, in fact, down to an electric reading-lamp) in the heart of Finland but to-day all these comforts awaited me, and many more. At the same time, there was a quaint mixture of modernism and the primitive, peculiar to this country, and not without its charms. Notwithstanding its up-to-date surroundings, the methods of the place recalled old coaching days, for the rosy-cheeked wife of the proprietor personally attended to my wants, and mine host himself waited at table, and like a Boniface of old, produced a flask of rare Bordeaux from an innermost bin in honour of his English guest. There are no huge hotels in Finland, none of the glare and glitter of the Swiss and Italian "caravanserais," where you are known as

KOPMANS-GATAN, TAMMERFORS

To face page 166

a number instead of a name. On the other hand, you will almost everywhere find cleanliness, comfort, and civility, and in continental palaces of travel the latter article, at any rate, is only too often measured by the length of your purse.

To give an idea of the kind of price prevalent at Finnish inns, here is the menu of a well-cooked and served little *déjeuner* to which I sat down on arrival at Tammerfors :—

SOCIETETSHUSET.

TAMMERFORS.

Nota.

	M.		P.
1 Bullion (Agg.) . . .			50
1 Chateaubriand (Potattia) .	1	:	30
1 Kompott . . .			40
1 Rodwinn . . .	3	:	—
1 Kaffee . . .			30
1 Cognac . . .	3	:	—
Total : Marks	8	:	50 p.

The "rodwinn" was an elderly (and genuine) St. Estephe, which would have cost double the price on the Paris boulevards. Three marks for Cognac is at first sight suspiciously suggestive of intemperance. Let me, therefore, hasten to explain that, in Finland, a *chasse* does not

consist of the usual *petit verre*, but of a
miniature bottle of brandy, which is usually
brought you reposing in an enormous ice-pail.
The bottle contains about half a pint, the whole
of which, once opened, must be paid for. Chart-
reuse and other liqueurs are supplied in the same
way, and this country appears to hold a monopoly
of the pretty little miniature flasks in which they
are served. My *déjeuner* (the last item deducted)
came to five marks fifty pennis, or about 4*s.* 7*d.*,
which, considering the excellent food and attendance, was distinctly moderate.

Tammerfors is essentially a modern town of
no historical interest, which in the year 1800
contained only five hundred inhabitants. It
was almost a village when visited in 1819
by Alexander I. of Russia, who was the
first to conceive the idea of developing its
resources by means of the almost limitless
water-power. Alexander II. also favoured the
scheme, and during his reign a few factories
were started and formed the foundation of
a now wealthy and prosperous city. Even
Finns admit that but for this ruler's aid and
encouragement Tammerfors would never have
attained its present importance as the third
largest town in the country, with a population of

over 25,000. That the place is yearly increasing in size is shown by the number of handsome stone buildings in course of erection on the outskirts of the town, which is characterised by the same neatness of plan on a small scale, as Helsingfors. I arrived on a Sunday to find the factories closed and the streets crowded with holiday folk. The Finns are a pious people, and on Sundays until midday the streets of their towns resemble a desert, for everyone, save dogs and policemen, is in church. During the afternoon the park, combined with a military band, seemed to be the great attraction. Here I found the *élite* and employees of the commercial world assembled discussing coffee and ices under the trees around the bandstand, and laughing and chatting in the shade and coolness, amidst fountains and flowers. Mill-owners, with their wives and daughters, artisans and factory girls, all were enjoying a day of rest and pleasure together with an utter absence of the prim snobbery that in any other country would have drawn a social line between the classes and caused uneasiness and restraint. As I strolled among the groups my own language fell upon the ear and I discovered that many of the mills and foundries employ English overseers. " They

call this Manchester," said one of the latter,
with whom I conversed, " but it ain't much like
it." The Lancashire lad spoke derisively, for
Tammerfors, with all its charming surroundings,
and high pay had no attractions for him. He
infinitely preferred his own grimy city in the
Midlands!

Wearying of the Gardens, I took his advice
and drove out to the Rapids of Nokia, about ten
miles distant.* A portion of the high road near
Tammerfors is used as a fashionable driving
promenade, and I was surprised to see really
smart and well-horsed landaus and dogcarts of
English build amongst the many droshkis and
country carts. Some of the ladies' "toilettes,"
too, that I noticed in this Finnish Bois de
Boulogne were evidently not home made, and
were set off by prettier faces than I had yet come
across in Finland. After a long and tedious
climb, the village of Pynnika was reached, whence
there is a glorious view of the surrounding
country. A prominent object here is a timber-
shoot, formed of rollers, where the logs are
hauled from the head of the lake system north of
Tammerfors over a steep hill (nearly a mile

* A pair-horse carriage there and back costs fifteen marks ;
one horse seven marks—but the former is best.

THE PARK, TAMMERFORS

To face page 170

across) and down to the waters of Nasijarvi.
Over a million logs cross here yearly on their
way to the steam saw-mills of Bjorneborg, on the
sea coast. The method was explained to me by
a cheery old gentleman who was sitting with his
family outside a cottage smoking and imbibing
iced " mjod." He spoke English, for like many
of his countrymen, he had sailed the seas of the
world. I questioned him as to the supernatural
powers attributed to Finnish sailors, and the
old fellow's eyes twinkled with merriment. " I
know," he cried, " my English mates on board
ship used to say that I had only to stick a knife
in the foremast to draw whisky from the water
barrel ! But it would have been no use to me—
a teetotaler !" I photographed the old salt and
his friends, but great disappointment was caused
by my inability to deliver the portrait, fully
developed and printed, then and there. " The
man who took that gave it to me at once," the
ancient mariner reproachfully observed, producing
a faded daguerreotype taken, many years ago, on
Margate sands.

Most of the way to Nokia lay through fragrant
pine woods fortunately free from the accursed
mosquito ; indeed, since leaving Imatrà these
pests had given me but little trouble and only

once appeared again, in anything like numbers, north of Uleåborg. Thus it was possible thoroughly to enjoy the drive through as lovely a bit of country as it has yet ever been my lot to traverse. Occasionally we would cross tracts of open land with glimpses of glorious scenery stretching far away on every side to the horizon, while, by the roadside, the quaint sight was afforded of newly mown hay, and corn ready for the sickle, in adjacent inclosures. But the sun was too strong to be pleasant, and it was good to plunge once more into the dim cool forest, where the sudden fall of temperature was like leaving the glare of an Indian cantonment to enter a convenient cellar. In the woods the profusion of ferns and wild flowers was remarkable, and I soon gathered an enormous nosegay in which wild roses, white and yellow marguerites, forget-me-nots, hyacinths, and a species of sweet-smelling lily mingled their fresh, fragrant perfumes. The wild flower of the north is generally a poor scentless thing, but these were an exception to the rule.

The Rapids of Nokia are nearly five miles long and rush through a narrow, picturesque gorge of a wild beauty, somewhat marred by a prosaic paper manufactory, which to-day was of course inactive. The mills are worked solely by

THE OLD SALT AND HIS FAMILY

To face page 172

water power at a spot where the rapids have been artificially contrived so as to attain a terrific force and velocity. Large quantities of paper of all kinds are made here and exported to all parts of Europe. We drove into the town again at dusk past the park, now gaily illumined by electric light, and down the principal street almost blocked by sauntering wayfarers. This thoroughfare is named the Kopmans-Gatan, or rather written so, for unless you pronounce the word "Chapman" no one will understand you. The Finnish Manchester is evidently not a dissipated place, for by 11 p.m. the moonlit streets were wrapped in silence and repose. I therefore retired early, and soon fell asleep to a lullaby common enough in Finland : the soothing sound of falling water.

It is said that when the North Pole is discovered a Scotchman will probably be found seated on its apex. This supposition engendered by Sandy's geographical ubiquity may or may not be correct ; at any rate, it is safe to assert that wherever mines or manufactories exist— even in the remotest regions of the globe—you will generally find an Englishman somewhere about on the premises. This was especially the case at Tammerfors, where, as I have said, many

of the overseers hailed from England. Even
the busiest quarter of Tammerfors is picturesque,
for the principal works are situated on the banks
of the foaming torrent that has made the place
famous. A fine bridge of granite spans the
river, and standing on its centre, you may look
away up stream beyond brick buildings, and
on to the blue waters of Nasijarvi, with their
wooded shores and peaceful islets, with nothing
but the distant clank of machinery to remind
you that such things as trade and labour exist.
Immediately below the bridge a tiny island
dividing the stream is occupied by a restaurant
once called the " Stromparterren," and famous
for a kind of sprat of delicious flavour. For
some unknown reason the " establishment " is
now disused and almost in ruins, for a pleasanter
dining - place on hot summer evenings could
scarcely be conceived than this rocky, spray-
sprinkled plateau. To your left, dividing lake
and river, is the villa of Mr. Notbeck, a wealthy
millowner, whose beautiful grounds are one of
the sights of the place. Near the gardens is a
large bronze eagle, commemorating the visits of
Alexander I. and Alexander II. to Tammerfors
in 1819 and 1850, and recording the services
rendered by these august monarchs to the town.

Looking down from the bridge, the rapids appear insignificant, and almost as though one could wade across them, and yet, once immersed, the most powerful swimmer would stand no chance. A few years ago some rash youths essayed to shoot the falls in a small boat, and were instantly swept away to destruction. A barrier is now stretched across the spot to prevent a recurrence of such foolhardy attempts.

The chief article of export from Tammerfors is paper extracted from the pulp of the pine and poplar. It is only of late years that this industry has developed into one of the highest commercial importance. Thirty years ago only cardboard and the coarsest stuff were turned out by very primitive means for local use, but at the present day *papeterie de luxe* of the finest and most expensive texture is produced. There are several factories, the largest of which employs about twelve hundred hands. Celluloid is also made in large quantities, and both products can be put on the markets at a far cheaper rate than if steam were the motive power used for their production. The gradual and steady increase of this trade is shown by the fact that in 1874 only a little over a million kilograms of paper were exported yearly, but now over twenty millions are annually sent out of the country—chiefly to England.*

The manufacture of cloth has increased during the past decade almost in the same proportion, and it is now made here of the very best (and worst) quality, for Tammerfors shoddy is a weird and terrible article of apparel. On the other hand, the finer materials appeared to be almost equal to those of English make, and tweeds, especially, are turned out with due regard to durability and good taste. In one of the cloth factories over 1,600 workpeople were employed. Schools for the instruction of this and other industries have been opened at Åbo and Helsingfors, and the labour is therefore skilled and up to date.

Time did not admit of my visiting all the mills, but if so minded I could have done so, for both owners and employees appeared only too willing to show a stranger over establishments of which they are justly proud. For paper and cloth works only form a small percentage of the crafts in this busy little town.†

---

* There are at the present time in various parts of Finland sixteen paper factories, thirty factories for the extraction of wood pulp, and eight factories of celluloid.

† The largest cotton mill employs 2,500 hands, and produces, on an average, nine millions of marks per annum.

ON THE ROAD TO NOKIA

To face page 176

Cotton mills, flax mills, and iron foundries are also to be seen, to say nothing of smaller concerns (also worked by water power) for the production of glass, china, matches, household furniture, beer, and aerated waters. I ascertained that labour is cheap—far cheaper than in England—for the limited wants and frugal habits of the Finnish working classes render them contented with a scale of pay at which an English artisan would turn up his nose. The latter receive quite double the wages in Finland that they would in their own country, which, considering the native talent at hand, seems curious. Perhaps the prejudice is due to superstition, imbued by the fact that the cotton-spinning industry was first introduced here by an Englishman, one John Finlayson, in 1835. Although perhaps 10,000 factory hands are employed at Tammerfors, strikes are unknown, which fact was now pretty evident by the open cordiality and good feeling that existed between capital and labour. There is nothing of the " sweater " about Finnish mill-owners.

Three or four days here convinced me that if Tammerfors is to be taken as an example of the rest of the country, Finland, from a commercial and manufacturing point of view, is going

2 A

ahead at lightning speed. Official statistics
show that in 1885 the total amount derived
from its industrial resources came to only 127½
millions of marks. Only ten years later this
sum was exceeded by more than sixty millions,
and it is now (1901) far ahead of that figure.
At this rate there is little doubt that in another
fifty years Finland is destined to take her place
as one of the most thriving and prosperous little
countries in the world.

NOKIA

To face page 178

CHAPTER XII

BUTTER—AND OTHER THINGS

THERE is in European Turkey a certain province (let us call it "Abou-Hadji") justly renowned for its tobacco, which is of so delicate and delicious a flavour that only very little of it is allowed to leave the country. The entire district is only a few miles in circumference, and, were the whole yearly crop exported, it would scarcely furnish a dozen London clubs. And yet you may travel throughout Europe, to say nothing of Asia and Australasia, and purchase any amount of this famous brand. You will find it everywhere, from Paris to Pekin, and from the bazaars of Bombay to the streets of Sydney. The consumption of cigarettes alone must be enormous, for they are sold cheaply in dainty, attractive boxes, notwithstanding the fact that in Turkey their price is almost prohibitive. But everything is in a name, and the London shopboy probably derives as much enjoyment from his spurious

" Abou-Hadji whiffs" (from Hamburg) on the deck of the *Marguerite*, as His Majesty the Sultan himself from the genuine article at Dolma bagtche.

And it is the same with the butter that the housekeeper places upon your breakfast table in London and placidly describes as " Danish." Here at least there may be some truth in the assertion, for the article of diet has probably passed through the country in question for the purpose of being carefully relabelled in transit. But the fact remains that of a score of cases sold by your grocer as " Danish " butter, two-thirds will generally be found to have hailed from some port in Finland ; for Denmark, like Abou-Hadji, is of limited area, and England is a large market.

This information was gleaned from the owner of a large dairy farm near Tammerfors—the same individual, by the way, who, when we parted at Tavastehus, invited me to visit his home—and I received a hearty welcome from my friend at a snug farmhouse, suggestive of Southern England, with its old-fashioned garden, creepers, and lattice windows, the latter overlooking fertile grazing ground, with sleek cattle browsing in the sunshine. Madame and Baby were absent, and we therefore lost no time, after a frugal luncheon largely composed of dairy produce, in sallying forth to inspect L——'s estate—or rather a portion of it, for the area was far beyond a day's march.

It probably comprised some thousands of acres, for although my host seemed rather hazy as to the actual extent of his property, the number of cattle from which he derived a more than respectable income ran into four figures. During the last twenty years the Finnish breed of cattle has been greatly improved (and the butter trade largely increased) by the importation of foreign cattle, chiefly from the Netherlands and Ayrshire. This, however, has only occurred in the southern districts, which are therefore far ahead of the northern provinces in all matters pertaining to dairy work. For instance, in the former there are now several large steam dairies, and their number is steadily increasing, while schools for instruction in cattle farming and dairy work have been founded in several of the southern towns. Every effort is made by the Government to encourage and further this branch of trade and exportation, and the State railways provide special milk and butter cars, heated or cooled according to the season, and carry dairy produce at almost nominal rates.

Southern Finland is admirably adapted for

2 B

cattle-breeding, and especially for dairy-farming, for the grazing is unsurpassed, while those essential articles, water and ice, cost nothing. And yet the Finnish dairy farmer has many serious difficulties to contend with, and perhaps the worst are the intense cold in winter and in

SMOKING OUT THE MOSQUITOS

summer the swarms of mosquitos, which in some districts render milking in the fields almost impossible. The neighbourhood of Tammerfors is fairly free from these pests, but even here it was necessary, towards evening, to kindle a number of bonfires around the homestead. I was puzzled by these strange proceedings, until I saw the cattle walk, of their accord, into the dense smoke, and stand quietly until the operation was over, when they emerged again into the fresh air, free to whisk and stamp away their tormentors. We strolled through some roomy sheds, fitted up with the most modern appliances for warmth and ventilation, and here, my friend informed me, the cattle are stalled from the end of September until the beginning of May. My host drew my attention to some ricks of fragrant hay and a barn crammed with roots and cereals hard by. "You see, we can afford to laugh at King Frost," he said, "although our hardest work is in the winter-time, and notwithstanding the greatest care and attention, we often lose many valuable milkers from the cold."

A stroll along a clear and rippling stream (where L—— told me he often landed a basketful of trout before breakfast) brought us to the dairies, a long, low building of spacious chambers, many yards in length, with ice chambers at intervals. A flooring and walls of blue and white Minton tiles lent a delicious air of cool cleanliness to the place, with its stained-glass windows, and double tier of wooden shelves groaning under great earthenware dishes of milk and cream. In one of the chambers a number of white-clad rosy-cheeked women were putting up a large consignment of butter for export, and I noticed that some cheeses were to accompany it, the latter as a present to some personal friends. Cheesemaking in Finland is a comparatively new industry, and one that may develop, but at present I cannot recommend the article, which in appearance only resembles an English Cheddar.

At present, however, Finland has as much as she can do to provide a grateful world with butter, and can well afford to dispense with a cheese trade. Most of my friend L——'s butter finds its way to England, sometimes direct, but oftener *via* Denmark, where it becomes, so to speak, naturalised and rechristened. It is landed in London as "Danish" butter, although it has rather less to do with Denmark than the oft-quoted "Stockholm" tar with the capital of Sweden. Some people are, perhaps, unaware that the United Kingdom imports some millions sterling worth of butter yearly. In 1894, for instance, the country received it to the amount of £13,470,419. One-third of this came from Denmark. The butter trade of Finland is now, however, quite equal to (if it does not surpass) that of the former country.* Statistics show that

* I take the liberty of here quoting the figures furnished by Mrs. Alec Tweedie, in *Through Finland in Carts*.

in 1874 about five million kilograms of butter were exported from Finland, while in 1894 this amount was nearly trebled, realising in this year over twenty-four millions of marks, or nearly a million sterling. Since then the trade has increased in an even greater proportion, for ice-breakers at Hangö and other ports now enable the product to be sent out of the country throughout the year, whereas formerly it was only shipped during the short summer season, and the waste was consequently enormous. Russia was once the best market for Finnish butter, but most of it now goes to England, and Germany is the next best customer.

An inspection of a steam dairy in course of construction was followed by a visit to the stables, for my host combined the breeding of horses with that of cattle, and some neatly railed-in paddocks contained a goodly number of useful-looking brood mares. The Finnish horse is presumably of Tartar origin. He ranges from 14·2 to 15·1 in height, and is a tough, wiry little beast, by no means fast, but well adapted for the plough and slow country work. As many as eight to ten thousand Finnish horses are shipped annually to Russia and Sweden, where they fetch good prices, but in Finland itself you may purchase a young and sound horse for from £10 to £12, and in the northern districts for even less. They are quiet and temperate as a rule, but very rough for saddle work. An attempt was made some years ago to import foreign blood from England, but the experiment was not a success.

The day was drawing to a close as we re-entered the portals of the farm, and the thought of a long drive before me suggested an immediate start for Tammerfors. But L—— would not hear of my departure until I had partaken of supper prepared by Madame, who had returned during our absence. "You will have but a poor idea of our Finnish hospitality," urged my host, "if I allow you to go away hungry!" So we sat down in his pretty little dining-room, with its tinted walls, proof engravings, and French windows opening on to the garden, to as dainty and well-served a meal as you could enjoy in the Champs Elysées; for the snowy napery, bright silver, and bowls of cut flowers were more suggestive of Mayfair than a lonely farmhouse in far-away Finland! Everything was perfect—from the dish of freshly caught trout that commenced the meal, to the wild strawberries and iced junket with which it ended. Indeed, the time passed so quickly amid these pleasant surroundings that night had fallen when we adjourned to the verandah for coffee ; and here, while enjoying a cigar amid the fragrance of a " starlit garden grey with dew," the subdued and silvery murmur of Madame's zither enhanced the silent beauty of the scene. Instruments should be adapted to their surroundings, for a piano in this weird northern star-light would have sounded as out of place as an accordion in Saint Paul's! Madame L—— spoke the French language and also sang charmingly, and when she had retired for the night I could not refrain from congratulating my host upon his wife's charm of manner and numerous accomplishments.

"Thank you very much," said L—— simply, "but it all comes natural to her. You see, she is a Karelian, and they are all born artists and musicians. Perhaps you don't understand," he added, noticing my puzzled expression. "I must explain. We have, then, in Finland Tavast-landers who live in the south-western parts of the country, and Karelians settled in the northern and eastern districts. Although both are Finlanders in the true sense of the word, the manners, customs, and even appearance of these two races differ almost as much as those of the people of France and Germany. The Karelian may indeed be called the Frenchman, and the Tavastlander the Teuton of Finland. In Karelia pleasure, music, and art are regarded as of far more importance than the more serious and practical walks of life. Our greatest poets and composers come from Karelia, where the women are famed for their beauty and the men are quick-witted, light-hearted, and totally unlike the Tavastlanders, who often appear dull and even boorish in comparison. Both have their good points, for although stolid and un-attractive, the Tavastlander is plodding and tenacious, and makes a better citizen than his clever but rather superficial countryman. As regards commerce, the former is the backbone of the country, for his word is as good as gold, and his perseverance unlimited. On the other hand, Karelians, while inclined to laxity in business matters, are neither thrifty nor indus-trious. Many are smart in business, but they lack the ballast and sterling qualities of their neighbours. We have a saying in Finland, 'Karelia for pleasure, Tavastland for work,' which aptly describes the situation. In the Savolax country (between Karelia and Tavast-land) there is a mixture of both races, and there you will find some of the most distinguished and cultured men in Finland."

"And you?" I asked.

"I am from Tavastland," replied L——, adding, with a smile, "I represent the commercial element in this household and my wife the artistic!"

It was past midnight before my hospitable host would hear of my bidding him farewell. My departure was delayed by the advent of a quaint but potent concoction (I forget its name), which appeared on fire in a large porcelain punch-bowl, surrounded by long-stemmed glasses. Rum was, I fancy, the chief ingredient, and a tumblerful was given to my driver, who had been peacefully slumbering on his box for at least three hours, awaiting my arrival with truly Finnish philosophy. The "yemstchik" of Finland is (unlike his Russian prototype) little used to strong liquors, and upon this occasion the unwonted indulgence of my coachman nearly led to a tragedy. For on our homeward way, while driving through the depths of a pine forest, a dark figure suddenly sprang from the roadside, seized the horses' heads, and brought the carriage to a standstill. "Robbers!" was my first thought, and I levelled a revolver. But the figure remained quietly at the near horse's head and gave no sign of molestation. Then I challenged it loudly, and the gleam of a pistol-barrel extracted a hasty explanation. The driver had fallen fast asleep, his reins were trailing along the ground, and the pseudo-highwayman (a wakeful shepherd by the roadway) had only just averted an upset!

Day is dawning as we drive into Tammerfors, past the park, looking deliciously green and fresh in the cool morning air, and down the principal street, where sleepy shopboys are taking down shutters, and street-cleaners are busy. We clatter across the cobbled market-place to the " Societetshuset," where I am confronted on the doorstep by a lad with a tin can. This is indeed returning home "with the milk," such an unusual proceeding in this staid and decorous land that I am regarded with suspicion by the entire staff of the hotel until my departure, the same evening, for Vasa!

CHAPTER XIII

VASA—NIKOLAISTAD

THE above are not, as might be supposed, the names of two towns, but of one city. If you wish to please a Finlander, use the first name, in which case, if a Russian be present, he will probably ask you whether you are alluding to the second! But anyhow, you may safely call the place Vasa, which is after all its historical name, originally derived from the great Gustavus himself. Nikolaistad was only an after-thought. In 1852 the town was entirely destroyed by fire and rebuilt largely at the expense of a prominent citizen of humble origin, but of great wealth. The combination is usually accompanied by love of notoriety and a hankering after the aristocracy. Nicholas II., then Tsar of Russia, graciously consented to a petition from the "Nouveau Riche" in question that the town should in future be linked with the name of His Imperial Majesty. And so it is known to this day amongst Russians, although every Finnish man, woman, and child in the place (to say nothing of the post and telegraph offices) adhere to the original title. If only for the latter reason, it is well to be aware of these facts.

Vasa is perhaps the prettiest town in Finland (which is saying a great deal), and contains about 15,000 inhabitants. The night mail from Tammerfors lands you here early on the following morning for the modest sum of about 12s., with an extra 3s. 6d. if you travel in a sleeping-car, an extra mark to the female in charge being most gratefully received, for, in these parts, very little money goes a very long way.

In Vasa nearly every street is a boulevard, and the town is almost surrounded by a beautiful park, a favourite resort in summer. Greenery is the prevailing note, for nearly every private house has its garden with shady trees and flowers. The public buildings are unusually fine, the roads excellent, with pavements of solid granite, and there are good shops and at least two very fair hotels. This is, in short, a prosperous-looking yet rather sleepy place, lacking the bustle and activity of the southern towns, which fact was apparent at the railway station, where only two cabs of antique exterior awaited the arrival of the train. These were promptly annexed by residents, so my luggage was placed on a truck and wheeled away by a porter to the Hotel Central, fortunately only a few yards distant. Here I found the restaurant already crowded and an atmosphere of "smörgasbord," roasted meats, and cigar smoke was not appetising at the early hour of 9 a.m. Tea and eggs were, however, brought me, the former a vile decoction apparently composed of senna and hay! Never drink tea north of Tammerfors, but the coffee is excellent, even on the borders of Lapland.

During the meal I noticed that Swedish was spoken by everyone, and that portraits of the Tsar and Tsarina were replaced by oleographs of the King and Queen of Sweden in the public rooms. I have said that the chief difficulty about the language in Finland is that unless a word is pronounced with native accuracy, no Finn will understand you, and Swedes are nearly as bad. In their language an egg is "ägge," which should be simple enough, but all my efforts to obtain one failed until a bystander came to the rescue. Vasa was in this respect the worst town I visited, and I had to resort, while strolling about the town, to my practice amongst the

2 C

Tchuktchis on Bering Straits—that of drawing my requirements on a sheet of paper. Thus to-day a rough sketch of a steamer lying alongside a wharf with steam cranes, etc., enabled me to reach the harbour, although verbal inquiries were invariably met by a state of perplexity.

It was a bright, sunny morning, but Vasa, although picturesque, is less cheerful and attractive than most Finnish towns, partly perhaps owing to the darker colour of the soil, which around here is the most rich and fertile in the country. This is essentially a grain-producing district, oats and barley being exported in large quantities, also rye, the greater part of which finds its way to Russia. This being an agricultural centre, there are many stores for the sale of farming implements of the most modern type, for steam is now largely employed for the cultivation of the land. A decade ago England furnished almost all the machinery for this purpose, but Finland now turns out excellent steel and iron work. In most shops of this kind at Vasa, two-thirds of the articles exposed for sale were home made, roughly, no doubt, compared with those from Leeds and Sheffield, but a marked improvement takes place yearly in this industry. A prominent dealer in agricultural implements assured me that, in a few years, there will be no market in Finland for English machinery.

The shops in Vasa are distinctly good, far better than those usually found in an English town of the same size and importance. In the principal street, for instance, you may purchase anything from an automobile down to a celluloid collar as easily as in London or New York, and at much the same price. The furniture establishments are especially good and up-to-date, and customers are accommodated on the " hire system." Booksellers are legion, for the Finn is a great reader. I gleaned that translations of the works of Mr. Anthony Hope had the readiest sale, but that those of Mr. Kipling were not appreciated by the reading public. Perhaps " Pro-Boerism " had something to do with this. At any rate, the immortal Dickens always holds his own, and of American authors Mark Twain is the most popular. Finnish literature is still in its infancy. It is difficult to name a really great prose-writer born and bred in the country, although the poet Runeberg is justly world-famed.

Midday seemed to be the fashionable hour for shopping in Vasa, and the main street then presented a gay and animated appearance, with its crowded pavements and brightly decked plate-glass windows shaded by striped awnings. The *coup d'œil*, however, was not improved by a large funeral establishment in its midst. The undertaking business is carried on here with greater publicity than in most countries, but the practice of exposing ready-made coffins for sale to the gaze of the passers-by is one that might well be dispensed with.

There is plenty to see in Vasa and to occupy your time for a couple of days. The town was founded in 1611, and therefore contains some interesting buildings, amongst them the old High Court of Justice, saved from the fire of 1852 and now converted into a place of worship, and the ruined castle of Korsholm. Amongst other sights the " Industrial Magazine " for products of local industry is well worth a visit, and here really beautiful souvenirs of the place in the shape of needlework, wood-carving, etc., may be purchased at a trifling cost. Perhaps the most striking object here is the Russian church, which stands on rising ground and commands a splendid view over miles of forest, field, and fjord. The size of the building is quite out of proportion to its congregation, for members of the Greek faith in Vasa are restricted to its Russian colony of under fifty souls.

The religion of Finland is Lutheran, but the influence exercised by the clergy over the people is infinitely greater than in most Protestant countries. Nevertheless, all creeds are tolerated, and I frequently witnessed open-air services of the Salvation Army, which has made great strides here during the past few years.

The port of Vasa is at Brandö, about a mile out of the town, and near it is the pretty beach of Sandviken, where there is fine sea-bathing and a good restaurant on the sea-shore. Brandö is beautifully situated, but its busy wharves, shipping, and gaunt grain elevators are rather a blot on an otherwise sylvan landscape. I strolled down here towards evening, when the pine-clad shores of the fjord were darkening against a glorious sunset and the blue waters of the harbour had faded to steel grey in the twilight. Work was over and the clank and rattle of winch and crane were hushed in solemn stillness, broken only by the ripple of wavelets against the pier and the notes of a concertina from the forecastle of a steamer moored alongside. The Swedish flag dangled over her stern, while a solitary individual on the bridge, enjoying

2 D

the cool air and a pipe in his shirt-sleeves, surveyed me with the lazy scrutiny of the seafarer,
and finally addressed me in English. He was
chief engineer of the small trading steamer which
I was presently invited to board, and which was
sailing that night with a general cargo for
Sweden, " which fact need not prevent us,"
added this friendly mariner, " from taking a
drop of ' Dewar' to the health of the old
country."

The speaker was of uncertain age. Snow-white
hair and a stooping gait suggested threescore,
but the twinkling grey eyes and vivacious manner
were those of a boy in his teens. My friend
hailed from Aberdeen, and had done most things
in his time : started life in a Chinese tramp,
managed a saw-mill in Alaska, driven an engine
in Peru, and a steam whaler in the Arctic, and
heaven knows what besides, finally drifting into
the Baltic timber trade, where he seemed likely
to remain, especially as, according to him, the
pay was good and life easy—and what more could
a man wish for?

Unlike most Scotchmen, my host was communicative, and half an hour in his cosy cabin
enabled me to gather much interesting information regarding subjects upon which he could

speak with authority. This canny Scot was well posted in all matters pertaining to maritime commerce, local imports and exports, and the carrying capacity of his little vessel, the *Carl XV.*, which dated from the early seventies, and was built from a model now happily extinct. But I was far more interested in his experiences of this perilous northern sea, which in the open season swarms with shipping, and yet across which, in the winter months, you may walk dryshod from Vasa to the Swedish coast. In summer dirty weather is rare in the Baltic, and sailors care little, at any time, for storms, given that most desirable commodity, sea-room. But this can scarcely be said to exist in this almost land-locked sea. Sweden bristles with defences in the shape of reefs and shores, while off Finland there are as many islands as there are lakes inland—islands of all sizes, from the dimensions of the Isle of Wight to barren rocks, just awash, that would not harbour a dog. And yet the eastern shores of the Baltic are not so dangerous as might be supposed. I had always pictured the mariner blindly groping his way through the darkness along the Finnish coast without bell or beacon to guide him ; but there are many portions of our English coast less

well and carefully lit than the western seaboard
of Finland.

Mr. Mac—"something" (his name has escaped
my memory) had twice been wrecked within the
space of ten years, but hastened to add that both
disasters had been caused by Swedish, not Finnish, carelessness. The collision with a Bjorneborg timber ship did not count, but the repairing
and consequent non-effectiveness of a Swedish
lighthouse were, according to my friend, unpardonable, although its extinction had been duly
notified in the newspapers. Mac was evidently
as "Pro-Finn" as he was "Anti-Swede," but I
afterwards ascertained that the information he
gave me regarding the pilot and lighthouse
service of Finland was unbiassed and correct.

The hydrographic survey of the entire western
coast from Nystad up to Torneå was carried out
by Finland (without any assistance from Russia),
and the task was one that entailed an enormous
amount of labour and expense. Little more than
a century ago Finlanders threaded their intricate
archipelago chiefly by the aid of landmarks
erected by the peasantry ; at the present day the
pilot and lighthouse service of Finland is as carefully organised as any in Europe. It has two de-
partments : one constantly employed in the survey

of coast and inland waters, taking soundings, making charts, etc., while the other consists of men actively employed as pilots and lighthouse-keepers. In 1897 the expenditure for survey work alone amounted to considerably over 100,000 marks. A few lighthouses of a very primitive kind existed at the beginning of the nineteenth century, but they were destroyed for strategical reasons during the war of 1808-9. It was only in 1831 that a light of any importance flashed forth its welcome rays at Söderskar, and other stations followed in rapid succession until the coast is now (as my Scotch friend put it) "as well lit as Regent Street!" And there is no doubt that a vessel need not coast here for many miles, after dropping one light, before she can pick up another.

At present the lighthouses of Bogskar and Market are the finest and most costly that Finland has produced. They are built on tiny barren rocks far out to sea, and their isolated position entailed an enormous amount of risk and labour. Materials such as granite, iron, sand, and bricks were conveyed to the spot by tugs and lighters from the mainland, and bad weather often put a stop to work for days together. The loss of life was, naturally, considerable, for the Market lighthouse is composed entirely of granite,

while Bogskar is of iron with cemented foundations of enormous depth. Bogskar was the
most costly undertaking, entailing an expenditure
of over 500,000 marks, while the erection of
Market cost the Government 200,000 marks;
and the money is well laid out, for disasters
on these fatal reefs are now very rare. In
former times as many as twenty-four wrecks have
occurred here in a single year, and eight of these
with the loss of all hands.

But these are not the only death-traps at
which the seafarer on the Baltic can now snap
his fingers, for there are now no less than 183
lighthouses (to say nothing of lightships) stationed
along the coast of Finland and amongst the
islands which protect it. This entails a yearly
expenditure of nearly 3,000,000 marks.* Several
lifeboat stations, with salaried crews and the
latest life-saving apparatus, are also to be found
wherever navigation is the least risky off the
shores of Finland, so that yachtsmen in quest of
pleasure need no longer hesitate to visit the once
justly dreaded Gulf of Bothnia under such careful
guidance and protection.

To turn to a brighter subject, Mac informed

* As yet only oil has been used, but it is now proposed to
illuminate the most important stations by electric light.

me that the most delightful sea trips may be made from Vasa, up and down the coast. Steamers leave here nearly every day during the summer for Jakobstad, Uleåborg, Torneå, and other towns ; or even Stockholm may be reached in forty-eight hours by the *Carl von Linné*, a roomy, comfortable boat, which leaves here weekly for the Swedish capital. A still larger vessel, the *Vega*, sails once a month for St. Petersburg, touching at intermediate ports, and a trip in this comfortable liner is a very agreeable way of spending a fortnight. For an excellent cuisine, a cabin to yourself, and civility from all on board (to say nothing of novelty and pure air) are seldom to be obtained for 16s. a day, which is about what the trip will cost you. Mr. George Bucht is the agent for both these vessels in Vasa, and it is better to consult him as to the dates of sailing than to trust to the local papers.

A worried expression on my host's face, caused by a sudden hiss of steam from the engine-room, hastened my departure, which my host did not attempt to hinder, for " time is money," especially north of the Tweed. As I was leaving the cabin a framed photograph caught my eye and arrested my attention, to the exclusion of some commonplace presentments of human nature and Scotch scenery that surrounded the picture. It was that of a young and beautiful woman, clad in white and classical draperies, crouching in an agony of fear, and endeavouring to ward off the ferocious attack of an enormous eagle which threatened to overwhelm her. The engineer noticed my glance, and winked blandly through a cloud of "Navy Cut." "That is forbidden ashore, but not afloat," he remarked, and proceeded to explain the allegory, which to the reader explains itself. It is said that the features of a late Tsar are cunningly worked into the plumage of the bird's pinions, but I have failed to discover them.

Electric lights were twinkling all over Vasa when I returned to my hotel after having watched the departure of the *Carl XV.*, and waved an adieu to her hospitable engineer. Nearing the town I found a crowd assembled in a field by the roadside, where a canvas booth flashed dimly in the lurid glare of kerosene torches. Hard by in a rope-inclosed space some weird-looking, oddly garbed figures were dancing to the strains of wild instruments. There were perhaps a dozen of them, swarthy and ill-looking, clad in scarlet, rusty velvet, and high boots;

AN ALLEGORY

To face page 204

while the women were of Eastern type, olive-skinned and almond-eyed, and wearing gaudy silks adorned with strange coins and barbaric golden ornaments. "Moustalaïnen!" whispered a bystander in answer to my inquiry, but I was none the wiser. Presently a strong man in pink fleshings relieved the dancers, one of whom, a villainous-looking ruffian with cork-screw ringlets, approached me. I addressed him in Russian, and his reply, although in a very different language, was intelligible. For I was acquainted with his birthplace (Temes-var, in Hungary), and told him as much in his own language. We adjourned to a tent, where I learnt (over straw cigarettes and a much-prized flask of "slibovitch"*) that this band of Gypsies had taken two years to travel from the banks of the Danube, by way of Austria, Poland, and Russia, to Finland, which is a very popular country with the Romany. For the peasantry are liberal towards these homeless wanderers, and my informant averaged £20 a week by his performances.

Having occasion to purchase a clasp knife, I strolled into a cutler's shop on the way home, and was offered one of Sheffield make for ten

* Hungarian "plum brandy."

marks. "We have much the same thing for three," said the shopman, adding modestly, "but it was made in Finland." As an experiment I decided upon the latter, which proved to be as good and durable as any article of the same price that I have ever bought in England.

By the way, an experience which befell me the same night at Vasa proved the versatility of

IN THE HOTEL GARDEN, VASA.

Finnish manufacturers in, at any rate, one branch of trade. "Eau de Vichy" figuring on the menu of the Hotel Central, I ordered a bottle for my supper, and it was brought me in a flask of transparent glass with a showy cork and a crimson label, as unlike the funereal flagons issued by the famous French spring as a bridegroom to a mute. Remonstrance with the Swedish handmaiden was useless. She simply showed her white teeth and pointed to the superscription, "Vichy Water" (Grande Grille) made by Messrs. Somebody and Co., Helsingfors. I had asked for Vichy Water ; there it was ! Argument was useless, so I sent it away, and bade the waitress bring me some Apollinaris, which also figured on the list. In this case, at any rate, the bottle was genuine, but it bore a notice to the effect that its contents had been manufactured in Vasa !

Surely human ingenuity could go no further.

CHAPTER XIV

ULEÅBORG

NO stranger can fail to notice the frequency with which the terminations "joki" and "jarvi" (pronounced "yoki" and "yarvi") occur in the names of town and villages in Finland. The reason for this is obvious, for "jarvi" signifies a lake and "joki" a river, and one or the other is invariably to be found in the immediate vicinity of city or settlement in this watery land. "Koski," "the falls," is also a very common termination.

Although the distance is comparatively short, the railway journey from Vasa to Uleåborg is a long and tedious one of nearly twenty-four hours by the mail. For the night must be passed at Seinajoki Junction, which was reached—leaving Vasa at about 6 p.m.—at ten o'clock the same evening. A start is made again at nine o'clock the following morning, and the train reaches Uleåborg at seven, so that there are only sixteen hours of actual travelling. In any case, the traveller must sleep at Seinajoki, no great hard-ship, for the hotel and restaurant are excellent, considering the isolated position of the place, which, before the railway invaded this lonely waste, was only a tumble-down village. The railway station now forms the nucleus of a pros-perous little colony, and the forests around are yearly receding under the influence of agriculture, which already shows great progress, considering that the Vasa-Uleåborg portion of the line was only completed in 1886. Two barrack-like, dark red wooden buildings accommodate the traveller, one being for second, the other for third class passengers, but I could see little difference in their internal arrangements, although, of course, higher prices were charged in the former, and its guests were also privileged to gaze upon the well-known belle of Seinajoki, Mlle. Elisa. Long before reaching the junction I had heard of Mlle. Elisa from some callow youths connected with the railway who never tired of extolling her charms. And she certainly was a pretty girl of the true Swedish type, flaxen hair, tall and graceful, and attired in a faultlessly cut grey gown that Doucet need not have repudiated. Nor was the lady entirely ornamental, for, in

2 E

addition to her duties at the bar, she did the work of three ordinary waiters at the dinner-table. When I ordered some Médoc she un-corked the bottle with such a winning smile that I had not the heart to send back the dark, mysterious contents, that tasted like watered treacle, and were labelled " Prime London Port "! You can rarely find a decent bottle of claret in Finnish railway restaurants, although it is nearly always procurable at the hotels, and the Govern-ment take good care that the public shall not be poisoned, for on more than one occasion my pint of " Margaux " or " St. Estephe " bore a notice to the effect that its contents had been analysed at the Government Laboratory in Helsingfors.

At the railway buffets drink beer or milk ; they are generally sound—at least, that was the advice given by Mlle. Elisa. Wishing to please her, I suggested, while taking coffee, that her presence would be better appreciated at a similar establish-ment in London or Paris than in this pine-clad desert. " I have lived in both," was the quiet reply (for this Swedish Hebe spoke English fluently), " and I did not like them at all !" " Well, why not Stockholm ?" I urged. " Because I prefere Seinajoki," retorted Mlle. Elisa, with a vivid blush that was only explained when I learnt, the next day, that she was about to wed an inhabitant of this dreary locality. The belle of Seinajoki's temporary preference for a secluded life was thus fully accounted for.

Travelling northward from Seinajoki the scenery

MLLE. ELISA

becomes wilder every hour. Few lakes are seen, and those of limited dimensions, for this is about the only part of Finland that is comparatively sparsely watered. The line is laid through large tracts of moorland rendered even more desolate and barren by the manufacture of peat, and the places where it has been worked stand darkly out against grey treeless plains thickly overgrown with heather and lichens, and strewn with great boulders of granite. Few natural products are wasted in Finland, and Iceland moss, which thrives here luxuriantly, has been exported of late years in considerable quantities to England and other countries as stable-litter. Here it is employed by the natives for the caulking of wooden dwellings, and its edible qualities have more than once proved useful in times of famine.

The train forges slowly and rather tediously ahead, although the engine is one of the modern American type, and, if necessary, could make much better time. But "Hurry no man's cattle" is the motto of the Finnish railway official. Talking of cattle, few are seen to-day, and the intervals of well-cultivated land are few and far between. In places the landscape savours of the near East, where perhaps a sandy plain surrounds us, with bits of bright greenery and golden grain surrounding the tall, wooden pulley of a well—for all the world like the "Shadoof" of the Egyptians. So the day wears away until towards evening, when the sea, studded with dark islets and flashing like burnished steel beneath a rosy sunset, appears on the horizon and tells us that our

ULEÅBORG

(Part of the Hotel in Foreground)

To face page 212

destination is at hand. And for the first time
the crisp, delicious northern air, laden with the
scent of pines, wild thyme, and meadow-grass,
steals in at window. To really enjoy northern
travel you must pass the sixty-sixth parallel, for
from here up to, and beyond, the Polar Circle,
the traveller will marvel in summer-time that so
glorious and health-giving a climate is not better
known. Other quarters of the globe may have
their attractions, but give me a summer in the Far
North, with its bright sunlit days and peaceful
grey nights, when the cold, clear atmosphere
braces and exhilarates the tired frame like champagne, and the smoke of a pine-wood camp-fire
is more fragrant than the perfume of roses.
" But how about mosquitos ?" the reader will,
perhaps naturally, ask ; and no doubt they are
bad enough, but a very minor discomfort compared to the climatic and other advantages of
a sojourn "up north." Anyhow, to paraphrase
a well-known poem, " If you have heard the
' *North* ' a-calling, you will never heed aught
else," for it is an undeniable fact that those who
have once learnt to appreciate it are invariably
drawn back, again and again, into the enchanted
zone by the same unerring attraction as that
wielded by the magnet over a toy fish.

2 F

When, in 1570, King John the Third of Sweden founded Uleåborg, he certainly selected an excellent site both from a commercial and picturesque point of view, for while, as regards trade, it is one of the principal ports of Finland, Uleåborg (which the Finns prefer to call "Oulu") is, next to Vasa, the most picturesque town in the country. The city of tar and timber contains about 16,000 inhabitants, and is of less modern appearance than the southern towns; the thoroughfares are clean and wide, but there is a quaint, old-fashioned look about the timeworn buildings and cobbled streets that recalls sleepy seaports on the east coast of England. Uleåborg is adorned with less greenery than most Finnish towns, and has no boulevards to speak of, but spacious gardens surround a new and large hotel, to which I was driven, and which fairly eclipsed (from outside) every "Societetshuset" I had yet seen. Indeed, until a giant in gold lace shouldered my luggage, I thought the driver had set me down by mistake at a Government palace of some description. For this massive stone building would have attracted attention on the shores of a Swiss lake, although tourists at these luxurious resorts might have reasonably objected to the accommodation. The

latter, considering the splendour of the uphol-
stery, might have been better, but as out of
a hundred rooms only four were engaged, the
management was perhaps hardly to blame. A
frugal meal, humorously described as "dinner,"
contrasted strangely with the gorgeous restaurant
in which it was served, and the footfalls of a
solitary waiter sounded ghostly and uncanny
in the dimly lit, deserted hall, which, notwithstanding its dark corners, was provided with
a music-gallery. But with this exception there
was little to complain of, for my sumptuously
furnished bedroom was suggestive of the "Ritz"
in Paris, and a blazing fire rendered it doubly
attractive, for the weather had suddenly turned
cold, and snow was in the air. "We are only
waiting," said the white-waistcoated manager,
whose sleek and prosperous appearance was
quite on a par with the rest of the establishment—"only waiting for the completion of the
railway, and this hotel will be crammed from
morning unto night." And as this white elephant
had already swallowed an enormous sum without
yielding one penny of profit, I could only express
my sincere admiration for "white-waistcoat's"
patience and philosophy, and hope, with him, for
better times.

But during the few days I remained at Oulu I saw little of its hotel. A letter of introduction which I sent the following morning to a certain Captain Hansen was immediately followed by a visit from that gentleman, who found me (at the early hour of 8 a.m.) discussing smoked salmon, dried reindeer, and *cheese*. This was the manager's idea of the early *déjeuner* I had ordered overnight, and expected to arrive in the usual guise of a roll and *café au lait*. But Captain Hansen expressed no surprise, so I presume this is a custom of the country!

I made many friends in Oulu, of whom this sturdy little sailor was not the least instructive and amusing, although a persistent habit of looking at the dark side of things somewhat affected the genial influence of his breezy personality. Hansen smelt of the sea, and you had only to glance at the man to know that he had passed at least five decades of his adventurous sixty years on salt water. But nothing he showed me of his native town (of which, by the way, he was extremely proud) was right or incapable of improvement. I firmly believe that should a benign Providence eventually land Hansen in the gardens of the blest he will complain that the grass is damp!

THE SOCIETETSHUSET
ULEÅBORG

To face page 216

Anyhow, my friend was a delightful companion, and time passed only too quickly in his society. There are many interesting things to be seen in Oulu, but our first day was devoted to an inspection of the tar stores at Toppila, about two miles from the town and reached by a small steam ferry, from which the clean, pungent smell of the tar was noticeable quite a mile away. A cluster of steamers lay alongside the wharf, waiting to load the endless piles of barrels, stacked under iron sheds, that extended for nearly half a mile along the waterside. My companion told me that 70,000 to 80,000 barrels are collected here every summer for exportation, which led me to remark what a terrible conflagration a chance spark from a ship's funnel might set ablaze. "Your countrymen saved us the trouble once," replied Hansen drily, adding that Finland had not yet forgotten this act of wanton destruction by a British cruiser during the war.

"And where does all the tar come from?" I asked, discreetly changing the conversation.

"Not from Stockholm," replied Hansen, with a sly twinkle in his eye; but I told him that I was already aware of the "Stockholm" tar and "Danish" butter frauds. I was not previously

aware, however, that the spurious name of
"Stockholm" tar is due to the fact that in
olden days the Finns were forced by the Swedish
Government to sell only to Stockholm traders.
"You may take it that most of the tar employed
in Europe comes from here," he went on, "from
the districts watered by the Uleåborg River;
Kajana, up river about sixty miles from here,
and on the further side of Lake Oulujarvi, is
the most productive district. But the tar trade
has greatly decreased of late years, partly because
timber has increased in value and partly because
the peasantry find agriculture and dairy-farming
more profitable. Messrs. Snellmann, who own this
wharf, now export yearly only about £30,000 worth
of tar, which is nothing to the business they used
to do. This year the South African War has
made it so difficult to charter ships that there are
thousands of barrels lying here idle. And it is
the same with timber, in which, in ordinary years,
Oulu does an enormous trade," and the speaker
pointed to a spot about a mile away, where
thousands of neatly ranged blocks of planks were
gleaming, like a small town, in the sunshine.

"But how is tar obtained in the first instance?"
I asked, confessing my ignorance.

"In much the same primitive way as it was a

A TAR-BOAT

To face page 218

couple of hundred years back. I believe there
are a few specially constructed furnaces up river,
but they do not appear to do any better than the
old system, which was simply to pile the wood
into a huge stack on an elevated platform, the
sole of which is bricked over. This slopes
inwards from every side to the centre, where
an opening leads into a vat under the platform.
The wood, after being thickly covered over with
layers of earth and grass, is then lit from below,
and slow combustion goes on for some days, until
by the sinking of the pile the top of the stack
falls in and a flame springs up at that point.
About ten days after ignition the tar begins to
flow, and is at once collected in barrels. The
best tar is obtained from the Scotch fir and
Siberian larch, but there are, of course, many
inferior kinds."

"And how is it brought down from Kajana?"

"In tar boats. There is one coming in now,"
said Hansen, as a wooden skiff, shaped something
like a birch-bark canoe, but larger, sped swiftly
down the stream. She looked perilously crank
under a freight of a score of barrels and a large
square-sail, but her sole occupant was a girl of
ten or twelve years old, who sat gravely steer-
ing with a paddle, and who had piloted the

rickety little craft safely through the troubled waters of Oulujarvi and down the foaming rapids of the Oulu River to her destination. I expressed admiration at such juvenile skill and coolness, but Hansen was, as usual, dissatisfied. "You are not much of a sailor," he muttered, "if you can't see that she has got that sheet all wrong." I eventually discovered from his cronies that one subject only was ever known to arouse my companion's enthusiasm— Butterflies, and upon this topic alone pessimism vanished and all Hansen's geese became swans. It appeared that the Captain had on a remote occasion, in the early sixties, returned from South America with a winged insect, which, although it had fluttered into his porthole one night by chance, proved to be one of the rarest specimens known to naturalists, amongst whom Hansen had ever after posed as a shining light ; and although his researches had commenced and ended with the capture of this much-prized moth, the proud remembrance of the fact had survived the chaff of years. "If you want to put Hansen in a good temper," said his friends, "talk to him of butterflies."

Before returning to the town an interesting visit was made to the house of Messrs. Snellmann,

situated hard by their business premises on the
wharf. The firm exports lumber as well as tar to
the tune of £60,000 to £70,000 a year. An
interesting plan in the chief office showed the
exports of various Finnish products at a glance,
by means of coloured cubes, the comparative
dimensions of which were also indicated by
numbers. Thus timber came a long way first
with a large yellow square marked "120," then
much smaller pink and green cubes for wood-
pulp and cereals marked "38" each; finally,
paper "28," butter "25," and tar "24." This
estimate was, however, for the year 1894, since
which the export trade in butter has greatly
increased. Most of the timber from here goes
to England.

English vessels are by no means uncommon
guests in Finnish waters. During 1897, the last
year for which statistics are published, 441 British
ships, with a total registered tonnage of 361,702,
entered Finnish ports. Of these, 434 were
steamers and 7 sailing-vessels. The same year
saw altogether 1,536 ships of other flags, with an
aggregate tonnage of 600,689, enter the ports of
Finland. Of these, 840 were steamers and 696
sailing-vessels.

The growth of the Finnish trade with England

in recent years is shown by comparing the statistics for 1897 with the corresponding ones of 1894.

The imports to Finland from England in the former year were valued at £1,169,484, and the Finnish exports to England at £2,045,978, against £682,485 for imports and £1,312,622 for exports in 1894; thus showing an increase for the former of 71 per cent. and for the latter of 58 per cent., or an increase of 61 per cent. on the bulk of the trade. This growth, enormous as it is when we consider that the interval is only three years, seems still more striking when we are told that there is an increase in the manufactured articles imported of from £250,547 to £617,763. In raw materials for manufacturing purposes the increase is not so large, although considerable, viz. from £341,005 in 1894 to £470,997 in 1897, or 38 per cent. Of the last-mentioned sum £177,160 was paid for raw cotton. Especially large is the increase in the imports of iron and steel manufactured goods, machinery excepted, from £87,341 to £237,152, or 160 per cent., and in machinery from £65,066 to £108,043, or 66 per cent.

Up till quite recently firewood has been cheap in Finland, and has been used for even mills and locomotives. Owing to the recent developments of the industries of the country, firewood has, however, become scarcer and consequently more expensive, and during the last year or two many mills and a number of locomotives on the rail-roads have been fired with coal imported from England. Thus, while the coal imports in 1894 were valued at only £51,781, they rose in 1897 to £119,317.

Among exports I have mentioned timber, butter, oats, and paper. The value of the wood export for 1897 was £1,137,121, that of butter was £653,119, as compared with £269,270 in 1894. Oats were in 1897 exported to England to the value of £119,204, and the paper and wood-pulp figures at £79,985.

If we compare the above figures of the trade with England with the corresponding figures of the trade with Germany, we find for many years past the bulk of the trade with the latter was considerably in advance of that between Finland and England. While, however, commercial rela-tions between England and Finland have been growing by leaps and bounds, the trade between Germany and Finland has been progressing at a somewhat slower pace, the consequence being that in 1897 for the first time the statistics show a large amount of business with England. And, as stated above, the bulk of the trade with England amounted to £3,215,462, whilst with Germany it amounted to £3,137,162. The difference is slight as yet, but there is certainly a prospect of a steadily increasing trade with England. I am indebted for these figures to the proprietors of the *Finland Gazette*, a journal up till recently published in London. It has now been superseded by the *Finland Bulletin*, an equally interesting, but rather smaller, publication.

"You would like a bath before dinner," said Hansen, as we stepped ashore at Oulu after a pleasant run from Toppila across the breezy river, which although so near the sea runs like a mill race. "There is plenty of time, for we do not dine till five," and leaving me at the door of a low whitewashed building, the little man bustled away to the club to prepare the meal and to collect some congenial spirits to meet his English guest. This was my first experience of a bath *à la Finnoise*, and I am not anxious to renew it, for to stand in *puris naturalibus* and be soaped from head to foot by a buxom lady (even of mature years) is somewhat trying to a novice. But this ceremony was apparently an essential part of the performance, and I therefore made no demur. The bathrooms were spotlessly clean and almost luxurious in their appointments, as is generally the case in Scandinavia, but the same cannot be said for Russian bathing establishments, most of which, even in Petersburg, are dirty and ill-managed.

I found a royal repast awaiting me at the club —an unpretentious but comfortable building in the centre of the town, with large reception- and reading-rooms, and billiard tables of the French type. Several guests had assembled at Hansen's invitation, and "smörgasbord" introduced some pleasant acquaintances, amongst them the colonel of a regiment quartered in the town, and an equally distinguished personage, Captain Ekholm, Director of the College of Navigation for the Merchant Service and founder of the Oulu Observatory. Our party also numbered a journalist connected with one of the three local newspapers and a Government official just returned from a salmon-fishing excursion, who had wonderful tales to tell of the sport to be had at Vaala. Thus champagne and wit flowed merrily as we discussed an excellent dinner, wherein delicacies such as smoked reindeer tongue and *laki* (a delicious fish only eaten, like the oyster, when there is an " R " in the month) lent a local colour

2 G

to the menu. And everyone spoke English, and if some were "pro-Boers" no one showed it. For at the close of dinner little Hansen produced and unfolded a huge scarlet "bandanna" with a portrait of Lord Roberts in the centre. "I drink to Bobs!" he said, rising with a stately gesture, and every glass was emptied. It was past midnight when we separated, and I walked home to my hotel in the pleasant moonlight, wondering whether there was another country in Europe where an absolute stranger would meet with such spontaneous and kindly hospitality.

Time sped rapidly at Oulu, for there was plenty to do, and the bright, sunlit days were perfect for excursions, although towards sundown a sharp nip in the air suggested furs. My pleasantest hours were passed at the house of Captain Alfred Ekholm, a man of culture and varied experiences, whose long and distinguished career in the mercantile navy had led to his appointment as Director of the Naval College of Uleåborg. Many a friendly chat did we have in his snug library after work hours and the departure of the pupils destined to join others now serving in ships all over the world. Other retired skippers would drop in for a pipe, and retail their interesting reminiscences in every imaginable quarter of the globe from Boulogne to Bering Straits and Archangel to Cape Horn. Captain Hansen was invariably present at these discussions, which he frequently interrupted with scathing criticisms, but the latter were generally received with loud laughter, for everyone knew that the little man's obtrusive cynicism was only skin deep. And so we would sit and smoke far into the night, which would perhaps terminate with a peep at the stars from the observatory erected by our host a short distance from the college, the students of which were thus practically instructed in astronomy. A certificate as mate in the Finnish Merchant Service is not easy to obtain, for the technical examination is much harder than in England, and a candidate must also pass in rudimentary surgery. This is scarcely surprising, for, as Mr. Henry Norman says, "Finland is a land of schools." The same reliable authority tells us that in 1890, out of a population of 2,380,000, no fewer than 540,412 attended school, which gives an average of 23 per cent. of the entire population actually under tuition. Uleåborg alone boasts of seven schools for the upper and middle classes, not including five for the children of the poor. A little incident which occurred in connection with one of the latter establishments is typical of the Finnish love of proverbs. It was related to me by an Englishman who while passing through Oulu some years ago made the acquaintance of a schoolmaster, now deceased. The traveller expressed surprise that Finland was permitted by Russia to retain her currency.

" Russia dare not take it from us," was the schoolmaster's reply.

"'Dare not'! Why, you could not fight Russia?"

"Oh yes we could; we make guns, and very big guns here in Oulu. We have an important foundry. Do you care to see it?"

The Englishman followed his host with surprised curiosity until they reached the gates of a large brick building from which were emerging a troop of merry school children.

"There, sir," said the Finn, pointing to the so-called arsenal, which was actually one of the largest schools, "there is our foundry, and there are our guns, at present on their way home to dinner! The weapons of my country, sir, are progress, civilization, and humanity, and let me tell you that in the end they will surely gain the victory over the deadliest engines of destruction ever forged at Cronstadt!"

For good all-round sport I fancy Oulu is

AFTER A DAY'S FISHING
ULEÅBORG

To face page 228

about the best place in Finland, for the Oulujoki
is one of the finest salmon rivers in the world,
and the fish are unsurpassed for size and delicacy.
The yearly yield for commercial purposes is from
eighty to ninety thousand marks, and this during
the very short netting season from the 10th of
June to the end of August. Kajana, on Lake
Oulujarvi, is the best place to fish from, for there
is a new and comfortable inn where rough
shooting may be had as well as excellent fishing.
At Vaala hard by are found sea salmon, sea
trout (Finn, "taimen"), trout and grayling, and
while the Kajana River teems with the two latter,
perch and pike are also caught there. Here you
may fish from the bank, but at Vaala it is mostly
boat-fishing. As a rule the same flies are used
as on Scotch rivers, and among artificial baits the
"Devon minnow" has been found very useful.
A permit for the season at Vaala costs only from
ten to twenty marks (this can be obtained at the
Tourist Hotel, Kajana), but without it you are
liable to a fine of one hundred marks. Kajana
is easily reached from Oulu, and on arrival there
the sportsman cannot do better than consult
Mr. Renfors, who, as I have elsewhere remarked,
is always ready to assist a visitor with practical
advice on all matters connected with sport. It

2 H

is well to remember that at Vaala the season
begins about a fortnight later than in Kajana for
grayliwg, trout, and gwyniad, and salmon are
biting in June and July, but the real season
commences in August.

There are many pretty walks and excursions to
be taken around Oulu, and, as usual, little
restaurants adorn some of the islets surrounded
by the seething waters of the Oulujoki. The
view up river from below the town is imposing,
but somewhat marred by a huge iron railway
bridge that at present leads to a railless embank-
ment. The principal churches are handsome if
not interesting, but I missed here a familiar
figure constantly met with in the south—the
" Fattiga-Gubba," or " poor man," a painted
wooden effigy, generally placed at the church-
yard gate, with a slot in his hand for alms.
The quaint and thrilling apparition on the next
page is to be seen on the road about half-way
between Tammerfors and Nokia.

An agreeable evening or two were spent at the
barracks, for I have invariably found Finnish
officers pleasant companions. The garrison of
Oulu was a small one, consisting only of 500 men
all told. Officers and men were Finns, and
although regimental bands had never been

A " FATTIGA-GUBBA "

To face page 230

permitted to perform the national air of the country, the Tsar had not yet announced his intention of altogether abolishing the Army of Finland. This will now shortly be done, and Oulu will make her first acquaintance with peaceable Cossacks.* Hansen was as popular at the barracks as elsewhere, and on the last occasion accompanied me there. Towards the end of the evening the conversation

* The new Military Service Law for Finland, which was sanctioned and signed by the Tsar on July 11, 1901, deprives the Finnish Army of its national character, which was guaranteed to it when Finland was ceded to Russia in 1809. In fact, this law does not recognise a Finnish Army at all. Natives of Russia may, without having acquired Finnish citizenship, under certain conditions, discharge their military service under the provisions of this new law enacted solely for Finland. Russian officers will get commissions in these regiments, which are now substituted for the national Army of Finland, and will acquire the status of Finnish citizens. The office of Commander-in-Chief of the Finnish Army will be abolished, as well as the Finnish staff, whilst the command-in-chief of the Finnish regiments stationed within Finland will be invested in the commander-in-chief of the Russian regiments garrisoned in Finland. Promotion of officers and of the rank and file to be non-commissioned officers will be dependent on a complete knowledge of the Russian language. The regiments, which are to consist chiefly of natives of Finland, may be ordered to serve, in time of peace as well as of war, outside Finland, within Russia, or abroad. The civil administration of the Finnish Army has hitherto been carried on by the military division of the Finnish Senate, but is now to be transferred to the Russian Minister of War. The Minister of War will also have the right to fix, subject to the Emperor's approval, the annual contingent to be called up for service from Finland.—*Times*, August 12th, 1901.

had turned on the police and passport system. Something had evidently occurred during the day to upset the little sailor's equanimity, for while walking homewards he inquired how often my credentials had been inquired for in Finland.

"Why, never since I left St. Petersburg," I replied.

"Then all I can say is that it shows great neglect on the part of the police!" cried the peppery little man, with a fierce tug at the bristly grey whiskers that boded mischief. But I deftly reverted to my friend's favourite topic, and graphically described a marvellous but imaginary moth supposed to be lurking in the jungles of Borneo; and when we parted for the night at the door of the "Societetshuset," all was peace.

ULEÅBORG

(Showing New Railway Bridge and Observatory)

To face page 232

CHAPTER XV ·

ON THE ROAD

I

SUMMER was drawing to a close. The coming winter had already shown its teeth with a blinding blizzard clothing Uleåborg with its first mantle of snow. A premonitory nip in the air warned me to get out of Finland as quickly and as comfortably as possible. How to get to Sweden—by post, road, or sea?—was now the question. Captain Hansen's remarks on the subject recalled the nigger's advice to the cyclist as to which of two roads the latter should select to a neighbouring town : " Which ebber one you trabels, boss, I guess ye'll be dam'd sorry you didn't take de udder!" But Hansen was a pessimist !

A small steamer leaves Uleåborg daily in the open season for Torneå, and takes about sixteen hours in transit ; but wishing to see something of the remoter districts, I chose the land route. You

233

may also travel by sea direct to Stockholm by a larger vessel, which leaves weekly and calls at Uleå, Sundsvaal, and other Swedish ports *en route*. This journey occupies from four to five days, and the price charged for a first-class passage, considering the excellent accommodation, is very moderate. The fare by the small boat to Torneå is forty kronas* first class and thirty-three kronas second class; but it is well to travel by the former, as the other is cramped and uncomfortable, and late in the summer squally weather often necessitates battening down.

My departure from Uleåborg was postponed for a couple of days in order to visit the prison—a really remarkable establishment—not that the delay was due to any difficulty made by the authorities, for most Finnish prisons are open (without an order) to the casual stranger. In this case, however, the Governor was absent, and I preferred to await his return before inspecting the establishment. The penal system of Finland is wonderfully well organised, both from a humane and industrial point of view, and a term of penal servitude here does not mean, as in England, perpetual degradation. I had opportunities (as delegate to the Paris Prison Congress of 1895)

* About £2 5s.

of favourably comparing the penal methods of
this to those of any other European country.
The gaol at Uleåborg was constructed to hold
two hundred of both sexes, but I was told that
it is rarely half full. On the day of my visit
it contained only a score of prisoners, some of
whom were females detained for petty larceny
and disorderly conduct. Social laws here are
very strict, and immorality is severely punished.
For instance, in one cell I found a woman
imprisoned for only six months for theft, while
next to her a homeless girl of sixteen was
undergoing a sentence of eighteen months for
questionable behaviour in a public thoroughfare,
imprisonment for which may vary from three
weeks *to as many years!* I was already aware
that sexual depravity is neither tolerated by the
law nor winked at by the public in large Finnish
towns, but the penalty inflicted in this case
certainly appeared excessive, and I was glad to
see that this juvenile delinquent was treated more
as an idle schoolgirl than a convict ; for her cell
was a large and airy room, comfortably furnished,
with a view of the country beyond the prison
walls. And the smiles with which the poor waif
greeted the matron suggested that the former

was perhaps better off, even here, than alone and uncared for in the cruel streets.

On the evening preceding my departure I was accosted in the restaurant by a seedy-looking person who suggested sharing my "karra" and

"A SEEDY-LOOKING PERSON"

expenses as far as Torneå. He was a swarthy, dissipated-looking individual, whose social exterior was not improved by a battered straw hat, a shabby black garment buttoned to the throat, and dirty canvas trousers much frayed at the heels. The man's nationality was dubious; he

THE OULUJOKI RIVER

To face page 236

had come, no one knew whence, and his destination was equally obscure. All the manager could tell me was that his guest had arrived with no luggage, and spoke five languages, which facts scarcely justified my regarding him as a desirable travelling companion. Siberia has taught me to distrust the wandering "papoutchik "* a trip with whom, in Russian Asia, often leads to unpleasant consequences. Urgent business at Torneà was the excuse given in this instance, but I politely suggested that the town in question could be reached in less than half the time that I should take by a steamer leaving in the morning. The stranger then departed, thanking me for the advice, and vanished through the doorway of the hotel and into the night—for good, as it turned out, and leaving an unpaid bill behind him !

This mysterious stranger may have been an exception, but as a rule the traveller need have little fear of molestation over any post-road in Finland, for most of them are as safe after dark as Piccadilly in broad daylight. A few years ago the roads west and north of Lake Ladoga had an unpleasant reputation as regards foot-pads, but the opening up of the country has made business very slack, even here, for the knights

* Russian " travelling companion."

of the road. It is well to carry (and display) a revolver in lonely districts, but, in all probability, you will never require it.

I have employed various modes of locomotion in my time, from reindeer, *à cheval*, in darker Siberia, to the Chinese mule litter of comparative civilisation, but I fancy that for sheer physical discomfort, not to say suffering, the vehicle by which I made the short journey from Uleåborg to Torneå is unsurpassed. I have never ridden a "yak," which may be worse, but I doubt it. Imagine a box on two wheels constructed to carry four persons, two abreast, and suspended at various angles according to the height of the horse. Viewed from behind, the axle protrudes on either side like the swinging booms of a warship, for no purpose, apparently, but to collide with every object within measurable distance. The cart is springless, and as cushions are rarely provided the occupant soon becomes aware of the fact. In other lands the monotony of posting has its compensations—in Siberia, for instance, when you are whirled along at full gallop by a "troika" of game little horses at a good twelve to fourteen miles an hour to the music of clashing yoke bells. There is some pleasure and excite-

ment about this; the pace, at any rate, is exhilarating, even if there be only a filthy post-
house at the end of the journey. But here
there was only one animal in the shafts, managed,
as a rule, by a surly individual with the most

AN INSTRUMENT OF TORTURE

elementary method of driving. We crawled out
of Uleåborg in drizzling rain, while a grey and
sodden sky gave no sign of improvement in the
weather. By the time we had covered a couple
of miles I began to wonder what devil's whisper
had ever induced me to choose the road in pre-

ference to a comfortable steamer. For an indifferent pedestrian could with ease have kept
up with my ramshackle " karra." Our ordinary
pace was a kind of amble varied by long intervals
of walking until the summit of a hill was reached.
Then, however steep the descent, the driver
would give a wild whoop, slacken the rope reins,
and away we would go at full gallop as far as
level ground, when the amble-walk business was
again resumed. It was necessary at times to
hold on like grim death, for the leaps and bounds
of the " karra " would have unseated a Texas
cowboy. Even at a walk the clumsy, creaking
machine rolled about like a pleasure skiff in a
gale of wind. Finnish horses are seldom vicious,
but are cursed with an inveterate habit of
stumbling, which does not enhance the delights
of a journey on two wheels, especially when
the post-boy is generally half asleep. I have
stated in the Preface that this journey may be
undertaken by delicate invalids, and so it can;
but they must hire a comfortable carriage at
Uleåborg and take it through to Tornea. There
must be no " karra " work.

Nearly a hundred English miles lay between
me and my destination, an easy day's work over
Siberian post-roads, but a journey capable of

being prolonged in these regions for over a week !
At least, this was my impression at Kolkarra, the
first station out of Uleåborg—a short stage of
about nine miles, which took nearly two hours
to accomplish ! Here the melancholy quadruped
that had twice bitten the dust on the way from
Uleåborg was to be exchanged for another—the
" karra " also, but we drove into the yard of the
post-house to find it deserted. Not a soul was
visible, indoors or out, and the stables might
have been empty for months. I entered the
house and found a clean and comfortable guest-
room, where a posting-book lay on the table,
and the usual menu of imaginary meals was
flanked by their Majesties of Norway and
Sweden on the wooden walls. But I summoned
attendance in vain, and when I emerged again
into the yard my driver had deserted me (I
had paid the stage in advance), taking the horse
and " karra " with him, and was already a dim
speck on the horizon, homeward bound. My
luggage and rugs had been thrown out anyhow
and were lying in the mud, under a pitiless
downpour. There is nothing like philosophy
on these occasions, so I dragged my traps
under shelter, returned to the guest-room, and
lit a pipe, to wait patiently for something to

2 I

turn up. And something did turn up, but only after a couple of hours, in the shape of the postmaster.

We surveyed each other at first in silence, for my knowledge of the Finnish language was restricted to a couple of words, learnt from Hansen: "Heyvonen soukala," which signifies "Get horses quickly!" The sentence, however had no effect whatever until a silver coin was prominently displayed to lend it force. My friend then rose and strolled out of doors and into the yard, where I followed and watched him as he stood in the rain scratching his head, apparently for inspiration. After a while he splashed through the mire to a neighbouring shed, from which the body and shafts of a " karra " were slowly and laboriously extracted. A couple of rickety wheels were then produced from another outhouse, and a shock-headed lout summoned from a hay-loft, where he had evidently been taking it out in slumber. Then a second instrument of torture was with some difficulty put together, and I waited with some interest for the means of locomotion, which had to be searched for, then caught, and then brought back in triumph from a neighbouring meadow. Finally, after a delay of exactly three hours, all was ready for my journey to the next station, Shippolara, and I took my seat by the shock-headed lout, wondering whether I might, with luck, reach my destination within a week.

The clouds now lifted a little, and clearing mists revealed a little of the country, which consists largely of wide stretches of moorland. The road (an excellent one all the way to Torneå) winds through wild, picturesque scenery not unlike parts of Scotland. Dark belts of forest occasionally appear on the horizon, fringing a grey-green desert with little vegetation but pink and white heather, wild berries, and lichens growing amongst granite boulders profusely scattered about the plain. Presently the sun shone out at fitful intervals, and my spirits rapidly rose under the genial influence of blue sky and accelerated motion. For the drive of a little over seven miles was actually accomplished in under seventy minutes, a distinct improvement on the first stage, and at Shippolara, which was reached at 5 p.m., a horse was actually forthcoming in less than half an hour! It is true the animal was unharnessed from the "karra" which he had just drawn from the next station to be put into mine, but, on this road, I had already learnt to be thankful for small mercies.

At dusk the little village of Virkulla was
reached. By this time the rain had again de-
scended in torrents, drenching me to the skin,
and here I resolved to pass the night. The post-
house here is the best on the road, but all are
good—under the circumstances, almost luxurious.
Posting facilities in Northern Finland are as
execrable as the accommodation is first class. A
decent dinner and a bed with clean sheets and
pillows is always to be had, even in the smallest
post-house, and the traveller will find every
reasonable comfort, with the exception, perhaps,
of Huttula, which was a very old building, shortly
to be repaired. At Virkulla the guest-room was
more suggestive of a private house than a place
of public entertainment. The floor was of
polished " parquet," bright as glass, and there
were rocking-chairs, flowers, and pictures, to say
nothing of a telephone to Uleåborg, upon which
Hansen rang me up during dinner to ask how
I fared. There was little to complain of, I
answered, for the postmaster himself prepared
the meal, which, to my surprise, consisted of
grilled trout, chicken, and a sweet omelette
served upon spotless china and a snowy table-
cloth—a pleasing contrast to Siberian fare,
where dubious eggs and sour black bread

generally formed the unappetising menu. My
host spared no pains to ensure my comfort. I
casually observed that the night was chilly,
and in five minutes a fire was roaring in
the chimney, pervading the apartment with the
pleasant fragrance of pines. The postmaster had
travelled, and spoke English fluently, and all
things considered, I can recall the night spent at
Virkulla with something more than equanimity.
When, the next morning, some delicious coffee
and fresh rolls were brought to my bedside, and
a bill for all these luxuries amounting to only
4s. 6d., I concluded, but erroneously, that the
reckoning was incorrect. And the posting itself
is as moderate. A horse costs fourteen pennis a
kilometre, or in case all the post-horses are
engaged, you may generally procure one from
the village for nineteen pennis (the legal tax). I
should add, however, that, in both cases, it takes
time! The driver is well paid at twenty-five
pennis a stage, but at these absurdly low prices a
larger tip is advisable, for it generally saves time
and ensures civility.

The postmaster was a pleasant and entertain-
ing companion, and we sat late over the fire
discussing local topics, while the rain pattered
against the window-panes and the wind howled

mournfully around the wooden building. I learnt that a good deal of the country around here is under cultivation, but that the timber industry is the mainstay of the peasantry. My friend was alone in the world, having lost his wife, while his only son had emigrated to the New World, where he was doing well in one of the Western States. His father was not an advocate of emigration, although he owned that his countrymen make good colonists. The fact that in America there are over thirty newspapers published in Finnish proves that. It is said that there may soon be a Finnish settlement in Vancouver Island, near Queen Charlotte Sound. The farming colony will be worked on a joint-stock and co-operative plan, and negotiations for land have for some time been in progress. Some enterprising Newfoundlanders have also tried of late to form a new Finland in their country, but the plan has not met with much success. Emigration, which has so rapidly increased from Finland of late years, was almost unknown before 1867, the year of the last great famine. There are now at least 150,000 Finns in America, most of them in the northern parts, where the climate so closely resembles their own. Ostrobothnia has furnished

the largest number of colonists, but every exiled
Finn dreams only of the day when he can return
with a sufficient competence to settle down
peacefully in his dear homeland. For these
honest, kindly people are as nostalgic as the
Swiss.

"Well, my own country is good enough for
me," said my host, adding, as if to change the
subject, "By the way, I have not shown you
my rifle." The weapon was a first-class one
of English make, and I heard the next day
that its owner was a famous "Shikari" who
had slain any number of bears and other wild
beasts in his time. And the bear in these
parts is an awkward customer to tackle. But
Bruin is getting scarcer every year, although
the forests of the north and north-eastern
districts still harbour a good many. The following statistics, published by the Government, of
wild animals shot in 1880 and 1896 would show
that the wolf and lynx are also dying out :—

	Bears.	Wolves.	Lynxes.	Foxes.	Birds of Prey.
1880.	115	321	301	4,229	3,509
1896.	91	15	86	5,265	7,776

As regards game and wild fowl, this part
of the country is well stocked with hares,

partridges, and grouse inland, and any amount
of wild and eider duck and wild geese on the
coasts. I could not hear of any snipe. Parts
of Finland are well preserved by shooting-
clubs formed in the principal towns, and it is
generally easy to get permission to shoot over
their ground. The close time for game is from
the 15th of March until the 9th of August. The
postmaster suggested the following as an ideal
sporting trip for both fishing and shooting
purposes : Helsingfors to Imatrá, thence to
Kuopio, on to Kajana, and down the rapids
to Uleåborg, and I have no doubt that he was
a good judge. He also informed me that a
paper called *Sport* is published in Helsingfors
solely for the use of sportsmen, but as it is
printed in Finnish I fancy that the average
Englishman would not derive much benefit from
its perusal.

The fur trade of Finland is, for a northern
country, insignificant. Thus in 1896, although
50,000 squirrel skins were exported, only about
1,000 ermine and half that number of otter skins
were brought in. The beaver here is extinct.
No less than seven kinds of seals are caught
on the coast, but only two are of any commercial
value.

"We had much better sport," said the post-master, as he returned from an inspection of the stables and threw fresh logs upon the fire, "much better sport before the railway people came here."

"The railway," I asked, "what railway?"

"Why, the line from Uleåborg to Torneå. It is to be completed in three years' time," and the use of some mysterious embankments that I had seen during the day (and taken for timber tramways) was explained. My friend was enthusiastic about the new line, although its construction was obviously not to his advantage, and from what I could glean the work will be one of considerable importance, strategic and commercial. But the difficulties have been great, for there are vast tracts of marsh land to be negotiated, and several formidable rivers to be crossed by bridges of steel, so that the entire cost of this comparatively short line is estimated at 12,973,000 francs, or over half a million sterling. The expenses are borne entirely by the Grand Duchy, only Finnish engineers and labourers are employed, and in, say, 1904 the traveller will be able to traverse Finland from end to end without the discomforts of the road or a small sea-going steamer. The passage from Torneå to Luleå will probably remain unchanged, for the new line is regarded with some suspicion by the Swedes, who are not likely to advance their railway system to meet it. Indeed, since the commencement of the Uleåborg-Torneå railway, a large fortress just over the Swedish frontier that had been dismantled and abandoned now bristles with modern artillery and swarms with troops.

At present the Englishman is a *rara avis* hereabouts, but I heard to-night of an amusing incident which occurred on this road a few years ago, of which a British tourist was the unwilling hero. He was a rude, blustering fellow of a type unfortunately not unknown to foreigners, and had, while fishing in a neighbouring stream, been the guest of the village pastor. The latter was rejoiced to see the last of his unpleasant guest, and the opportunity occurring, resolved to pay him out for at least some of the discomfort caused by his prolonged visit. " Tell me a good Finnish oath, parson," said the Briton as he entered the post - cart for the first stage of his journey. " These post-boys are lazy dogs," and the required information was smilingly imparted. Now it so happened that the driver was unusually dull and boorish, and the native swear-word was shortly put into requisition. " Drive faster, you idiot! Do you hear? Drive faster!" cried the irate passenger, and the order producing no effect, he seized the man's collar and shook him violently, shouting, "'Rakastansunia!' you silly dolt; 'Rakastansunia!'" The result was magical, for with a wild stare of horror the man dropped the reins, leapt out of the "karra," and made tracks across country at a speed that defied pursuit. After a long and weary trudge the tourist discovered him at the nearest post-house in earnest conclave with the postmaster, whose perplexed features relaxed with a broad grin of relief when the details of the affair had with some difficulty been explained. "Rakastansunia!" he repeated, bursting into roars of laughter. "No wonder the poor boy took you for a lunatic and fled for his life. Why, 'Rakastansunia' means 'I love you'!"

Midnight was striking from an asthmatic cuckoo clock when I rose to retire to my sleeping-place, the outline of which flashed cosily from a dark recess in the rays of the now expiring fire. A somewhat gaudy banner was suspended over the bedstead. "The flag of Finland?" I asked, pointing to the strip of blue and white bunting.

"Finland has no flag—never had one," gravely

replied my host. "Those are the colours of my club at Åbo. Our national emblem has always been that of Sweden or Russia. But we do possess a coat‑of‑arms," added the old man proudly, "a coat-of-arms presented to us in 1583 by King John of Sweden for a great and glorious victory, and that is better than any flag."*

"You should stop over to-morrow," said my host, as he barred the door for the night, and I clambered into soft and inviting sheets, "for I have a 'talkoo.'"

"And what is a 'talkoo'?" I asked sleepily, for a long day's posting in the rain is worth pints of chloral.

"Simply a Finnish custom, and a very useful one, that dates from the Middle Ages. It illustrates your English proverb: 'One good turn deserves another.' To-morrow I am doing some small repairs to the stables. Some thirty of my neighbours will arrive in the morning, and after a good meal set to work. At the end of the day I shall provide a supper, and the young people will dance. It is turning toil into pleasure, but very profitable pleasure, for in this way the work of twelve days is often got through in as many hours. Next week I assist at the talkoo of a

* The arms of Finland appear on the cover of the volume.

friend—he is getting in his harvest—and so we go on." But I had already gone on—to the land of dreams, and my worthy friend's concluding remarks fell upon heedless and ungrateful ears.

with all the skill and assurance of an old stager.
He used no whip—the post-boys here never do—
for throughout Finland the kindness of the people
to animals is proverbial. It was occasionally
almost exaggerated, as in the case of an old
market woman I saw one day in the streets of
Uleåborg. The sky was overcast and the temperature decidedly chilly, but she had carefully
provided her pony with a sun-bonnet! This
was the only equine head - dress that I saw
throughout the country, and perhaps the good
lady was under the impression that it was less
for use than ornament!

Most of the journey to-day lay through pine
forests, with occasional clearings of arable and
pasture land. During the first stage a river of
considerable size was crossed by means of a
chain-ferry. The ferryman's cottage was on the
further side of the stream, perhaps a quarter of
a mile across, and an original method of attract-
ing his attention was by means of a rope
stretched across the river like a telegraph wire
and attached to a bell in his hut. A white flag
in the branches of a pine tree indicated the bell-
pull.

The rain had ceased, leaving the valleys
shrouded in mist so dense that my furs were

wringing wet on arrival at Tolonen, a pretty little place of some dozen houses about twelve English miles from Virkulla. Tolonen was perhaps the most picturesque village on the road, but all were laid out with a neatness and regularity worthy of imitation in more civilised lands. Here, as in the south, dark red is the

A MEMBER OF THE HUMANE SOCIETY

prevailing colour of the wooden dwellings, but doors and windows are picked out with white in Swedish style, which relieves to a certain extent the sombreness of their exterior. Every post-house I entered was built upon the same plan, and consisted of three separate buildings at right angles, inclosing a yard, and formed by the residence, granary, and stables. Most of the

2 L

farms are one-storied, although occasionally an upper floor may be reached by an outer stairway. A bathroom is invariably found attached to the humblest homestead, where vapour is produced *à la Russe* by pouring water on red-hot bricks, while the bathers birch themselves into a profuse perspiration. A cold plunge into a snowdrift is, in winter, the concluding operation, while in summer there is generally a lake or river handy. Some years ago the sexes here bathed together, as in Japan, but this practice is now obsolete. A bath-house is used at times for other than cleansing purposes, a fact of which, nearing Torneå, I was unpleasantly made aware. Being about to enter one of these buildings, I was warned by a bystander to keep away, as it contained a small-pox patient! When no hospital is available fever cases are generally isolated in this way. Infectious diseases are, however, very rare here. Pulmonary complaints are the chief cause of mortality, while, for some unknown reason, Finland contains, for its size, more blind people than any country in the world, Egypt perhaps excepted. On the other hand, the Grand Duchy is far ahead, even of the United Kingdom, as regards lunacy statistics, for out of a million Finns only 1,700 are insane, and no part of

A FERRY NEAR TOLONEN

To face page 258

England drops below 2,500, London heading
the list with 3,610 lunatics in each of her five
millions!

The Finnish peasantry have now no distinctive dress. The men generally wear rough
tweeds, or in summer-time linen blouses secured
round the waist by a leather belt. High boots
called "pjaksor" are the usual footgear—a kind
of soft, soleless moccasin, turned up at the toe.
The women affect bright-coloured cotton bodices,
while their skirts and aprons are generally neatly
embroidered. Very few wear ornaments, and
the national head-dress consists of an unbecoming
blue or crimson handkerchief, tied anyhow under
the chin. Comely faces are often seen south of
Uleåborg, but north of this town a good-looking
woman is a rarity, although even here the
children of both sexes are generally pretty and
attractive, and, as a school is usually within easy
reach, intelligent as well. The prosperity of the
Finnish peasant is probably largely due to his
enforced sobriety, for the sale of alcohol is
strictly forbidden in the villages, and even a
well-to-do farmer can only obtain intoxicating
liquor by going to the principal town of his
district, which is often a considerable distance
away. And Hodge is here as frugal as he is

sober. Meat rarely enters into the daily fare, which consists of salt fish, porridge, milk, and a kind of biscuit made of rye, so hard that it will almost defy the strokes of a hammer. Coffee is the favourite beverage, and in hot weather "kalja," a kind of beer resembling the Russian "kvas," which, when iced, is harmless and very refreshing.

The Finnish peasant, unlike his Russian neighbour, generally takes a very serious view of life, and he is not, as a rule, an attractive personage, being shy, reserved, and even surly with strangers, although his courage, sincerity, and hospitality more than atone for these social defects. The Russian Moujik is a merry, roystering fellow, especially when in his cups, but the Finn rarely indulges in boisterous mirth, preferring, even on festive occasions, to take his pleasure sadly. It was formerly the custom to weep at weddings and rejoice at a funeral, which indicates his morbid proclivities. The long winter nights must pass drearily enough here, for games of cards or chance are seldom found in farm or cottage. A favourite method of killing time is for a number of neighbours to gather round a fireplace and propound riddles, of which the following are examples: Q. "What is as old as

the earth and yet not five weeks of age?"
A. "The moon." *Q.* "What is it that cannot
speak, yet tells the truth to the whole world?"
A. "A pair of scales," etc. One can well imagine
that the silence of despair would almost be pre-
ferable to listening, for any length of time, to
conundrums of this kind.

At Tolonen there was not a horse to be had
for love nor money, so I passed most of the day
there in enforced inactivity, gleaning the above
facts from the postmaster, who had lived in
"Pietari" (as Petersburg is called in Finland)
and spoke Russian fluently. Arriving at midday, I was detained here for nearly seven hours
before proceeding on my journey, and only
reached Huttula after dark. And here a similar
experience to that of Kolkarra awaited me, for
the post-house door was securely barred and
the whole dwelling wrapped in silent darkness.
After several ineffectual attempts to obtain ad-
mittance, the driver joined me in a series of
yells that would have aroused the seven sleepers,
but only awakened a responsive chorus from
some curs in the distance. Finally a bright
idea struck my companion, who, before I could
restrain him, had hurled a huge stone through
a double window of the guest-room. Then,

2 M

at last, the resounding crash of breaking glass brought the welcome sound of drawn bolts and the sight of a dirty, dishevelled female to the door. This unlovely apparition was the only occupant, and having ascertained that horses were out of the question until the morning, I sought a sleeping-place, and found, in the guest-room, a bedraggled bed, apparently just vacated by the damsel in question. The latter promptly disappeared, for her costume was of the scantiest description, and our nocturnal invasion had scared her into a condition of hopeless idiocy. So the post-boy brought in my traps, and before his departure lit a fire, for the night was cold, and the ground white with hoar-frost.

If at Tolonen there had been a dearth of horses, Huttula could at any rate boast of a plague of rats, some of them of unusual size and audacity, and I passed a wakeful and miserable night. Not only was the guest-room infested with these repulsive brutes, but I was also attacked by swarms of mosquitos, which, considering the low temperature, was curious. Oddly enough, Huttula was the only place on the road where I missed a mosquito bar, but the village is surrounded by marshes, which probably accounted for the temporary discomfort.

Fortunately I was provided with candles, and read until daylight, when the enemy retired from the scene and left me to slumber in peace.

The postmaster only returned at 9 a.m., but an hour later I was again *en route* with a horse hired from the village. There was no driver available, so I gladly agreed to a suggestion that I should, myself, act as post-boy. The

SWEET REPOSE

stage was a short one, but the horse was less tired than the coachman at its conclusion, for to drive a Finnish post-horse is infinitely more fatiguing than to ride double the distance on Shanks's mare! There was, perhaps luckily, no river work to speak of, and Riukkala was reached in fairly good time. Here I found horses, but

not a man about the station, only a stout and
garrulous old lady, who informed me that all
were out at work in the fields. I therefore
resignedly prepared for another long and tiresome delay, when the old dame waddled off to
the stables and presently returned with a horse
and "karra." Scrambling with difficulty into
the cart, she beckoned me to follow, which I
did, to be driven out of the yard, and, for quite
half the stage, at a hand gallop. For this female
post-boy evidently knew her business, although
her driving was occasionally rather more daring
than artistic.

At Maroshemakki, the next station, I was
given to understand that when I arrived at Kemi,
a small town on the Gulf of Bothnia, a short
journey of four or five miles thence would land
me at Torneå. I drove into Kemi well before
sundown, and having plenty of time to spare,
entered the post-house, and ordered refreshment,
intending to travel on leisurely, and reach
Torneå by dinner-time. The post-house at
Kemi (which, by the way, is the smallest town
in Finland) is almost an hotel, with excellent accommodation, and I should have done
well, as events turned out, to have passed the
night there. But the place itself is a dismal hole

of some four hundred inhabitants (mostly engaged in the timber trade), and offered no inducements for a prolonged stay. There is a curious old church of the sixteenth century, which is about all there is worth seeing. Coffee and cakes having therefore been discussed, I lit a cigar, and took my seat with the pleasant reflection that the journey was now practically over, the more so that a wiry little horse in the shafts raced along and tore at his bridle in a way that looked like landing me at my final destination within the half-hour.

The little town of Kemi stands at the southern extremity of a large plain bisected by the Kemi River, which rises in Lapland and runs a course of about a hundred miles through a fertile and well-wooded country before it joins, near the town of its name, the Gulf of Bothnia. The scenery here is attractive in summer, for snug homesteads are seen in neatly inclosed pastures, watered by the blue and winding river, while cattle and tinkling cowbells lend a homely and peaceful aspect to a scene which in winter must be one of howling desolation. For then verdure and vegetation are merged in a white and pathless world, and as the forests here afford scanty protection, there is nothing

to break the force of the blizzards that sweep
down, with relentless fury, from the Arctic.
Even in June a cloudless sky is sometimes
darkened, and the thermometer drops thirty or
forty degrees in a couple of hours, playing sad
havoc with the crops.   By the way, a pleasant but
rather difficult summer trip may be made by taking
one of the "Midnight Sun" steamers to North
Cape, in Norway, and travelling thence through
Finland to Kemi by the Tàna, Kittilä, and Kemi
Rivers.   But the journey, which occupies about
a fortnight, is a tough one, that should only be
undertaken by those accustomed to "rough it"
in the worst sense of the word.   There are also
numerous and dangerous rapids, which render
the voyage, in parts, rather risky.   On the other
hand, the trip costs only about £25 from sea to
sea, and the fishing alone is well worth the
money. Captain Pulley, R.N., the well-known
explorer, visited the Tàna country a few years
ago, and obtained excellent sport.   He tells me
that he landed, within a few days, one hundred
and twenty-three salmon, averaging twenty
pounds apiece. Big spoon and minnow were used
for high water, and, for a low river, "Durham
Ranger," "snow fly," and especially "black and
silver," were the best. My informant found

satisfactory but, of course, very primitive accommodation in parts of the Tanà district, and was everywhere received with hospitality.

When we left Kemi the sun was still high in the heavens, but it was dipping below the horizon when I looked at my watch, to find that, although we had travelled for an hour at a fair pace, there was as yet nothing to show that we were nearing Torneå. Indeed, the country seemed to become wilder and more desolate, and I vainly searched the rapidly darkening landscape for signs of human habitation. The driver, at first, seemed an intelligent youth, but when questioned appeared very hazy as to the position of Torneå, the name of which I repeated while pointing to the dial of my watch. " Torneå!" I cried. "What time get Torneå?" in the broken English generally used, for some occult reason, by the Briton abroad. But the mysterious word " Mikkola" was the only reply, accompanied by a vacant smile, which, under the circumstances, was intensely irritating. And the smile became broader and blander as my impatience increased, but my companion remained unruffled, occasionally murmuring " Mikkola" in a silly, mechanical tone that, after a while, inclined me to the belief that the speaker was not quite right

in his head. For we had already come at least
ten miles from Kemi, which is distant only five
miles from Torneå, and the probability must
therefore be that we were going in a directly
opposite direction. What a fate! To be stranded
in a wild and unknown country at nightfall, at
the mercy of a mad post-boy!

There was nothing for it, though, but to sit
tight and trust to luck and a safe arrival at
Mikkola, wherever that might be. And at last
patience was rewarded, for a glitter of lights in
the distance set my mind at rest, at any rate, as
to my guide's sanity. "Mikkola," he murmured,
pointing to the friendly beacon, and we pulled up
shortly afterwards in front of a large and well-lit
post-house, after a stage of exactly an hour and
twenty minutes out from Kemi.

The postmaster was smoking with some
acquaintances on the doorstep. "I want to go
to Torneå," I cried, but my demand was met
by a dull stare of surprise. "Hey vonen
Soukkala—Torneå!" I repeated, and the man
nodded silently, evidently astonished at my
vehemence. Not a soul in the place spoke
a word of Russian, and I might as well have
questioned a New Zealander in Turkish as anyone here as to my whereabouts. But a "karra"

was prepared, which induced me to conquer my hesitation, and to urge once more upon my wild career. "Torneå?" I shouted, interrogatively, as we drove away in the darkness, but the post-master only turned away, and I saw him rejoin his friends with a laugh and a shrug of his shoulders. He probably took me for a wandering lunatic, or for very much the same thing in the minds of most foreigners, an eccentric Englishman!

It was now as dark as a tunnel, and a drizzling rain was falling. When we had reached the banks of a wide and swollen river (the Kemi, as I afterwards discovered) the inclination seized me to abandon the journey and return, in despair, to Kemi. But the river was crossed in the usual way by a chain-ferry, and midway across some floating logs struck us heavily amidships, heeling the boat over for a moment at a very awkward angle. When, therefore, land was reached, I resolved, after this unpleasant incident, to sleep on this side of the stream.

A long and miserable drive followed. The post-boy was a patriarchal individual, who stubbornly refused to reply even by signs to my inquiries. For over an hour we laboured across a bleak and barren tract of country through pouring rain, which a cold, gusty wind rendered doubly disagreeable. Finally I fell into a fitful slumber, to awaken with a start on the shores of yet another river, almost an arm of the sea it appeared, with great white rollers gleaming out of the night, and breaking with a roar upon the sandy beach. But my soul was comforted, for the lights of streets and buildings were visible across the water. It was now blowing half a gale, and the ferry rolled like a ship in dirty weather, but although an icy blast cut through clothes that clung to me like a wet bathing suit, I bore these minor discomforts with equanimity, for a town of this size could only be the one I was in quest of.

It was past midnight when I at length sat down to a very welcome repast at the Staats Hotel, an unpretentious but comfortable house. "Well, that is the longest five miles I ever travelled in my life," I observed to the land-lord, referring to the weary drive from Kemi· "I don't know," was the reply; "it is an easy journey. Of course you know that they are *Swedish* miles, one of which is equal to four of your English ones!" As a matter of fact, I knew nothing of the kind, but not wishing to display my ignorance, said no more.

The following list of post-stations between Uleåborg and Torneå, and the approximate length of the stages, is given for the benefit of travellers.

Kilometres.*

Uleåborg to Kolkarra .	14	*Bad Post-house*
Kolkarra to Shippolari .	12	
Shippolari to Soronen .	14	
Soronen to Virkulla .	12	*Good Post-house*
Virkulla to Tolonen .	20	
Tolonen to Huttula .	18	*Bad Post-house*
Huttula to Riukkala .	12	*Good Post-house*
Riukkala to Maroshemakki	16	
Maroshemakki to Kemi .	14	*Good Post-house*
Kemi to Mikkola . .	10	*Good Post-house*
Mikkola to Vallo . .	10	
Vallo to Torneå . .	20	

* Ten kilometres is about six English miles.

AT KEMI

CHAPTER XVII

TORNEÅ, LULEÅ, STOCKHOLM

TORNEÅ (pronounced Torne–"*o*,") is a straggling, dreary-looking little town of some thousand inhabitants. The reader has perhaps noticed a tiny circle surmounting the first letter of the alphabet in such names as Åbo, Borgå, and Åland. This means that the "a" is to be spoken as an "o." The practical mind may not unnaturally reason that a single "o" might well, in this case, serve the same purpose, but there is perhaps some subtle reason for the dual combination, for in Sweden it is the same, as witness Luleå, Piteå, Urmeå, and several other towns. It would seem to be the object of the Finlander to puzzle the stranger within his gates (from a geographical point of view) as much as possible, for there is scarcely a town of any importance in the country that does not bear a double name. Take, for instance, Helsingfors

THE TORNEÅ RIVER IN SPRING-TIME

To face page 272

(Helsinki), Tammerfors (Tampere), Uleåborg (Oulu), and many others too numerous to mention. In some cases the dissemblance is complete, as, for example, Åbo, which is also known as "Turku." I may mention that this city is scarcely ever alluded to by the latter name, and why, therefore, should it exist? But the Finns are a conservative people.

Torneå (the most northerly town in Finland) is situated at the head of the Gulf of Bothnia, on the Russo-Swedish frontier. It is separated from the Swedish town of Haparanda by the River Torneå, the two places being connected by a long, but rickety, wooden bridge. The broad shallow stream which forms the boundary is here nearly a mile broad, and, in dry seasons, one may almost wade across, although the spring floods sometimes convert it into a foaming torrent. In winter this river presents an appearance so desolate, and yet so picturesque, that it is here shown as photographed just before the break-up of the ice in the month of March.

Torneå dates from 1605, but is an un-attractive, uninteresting place, which, before its annexation by Russia in 1809, carried on a con-siderable trade with Stockholm. But it is now the picture of desolation, with untidy wooden

buildings, grass-grown streets, and a sleepy population, most of whom were chiefly employed in
lounging about the streets and in and out of the
Staåts Hotel, where "smörgasbord" was going in
the restaurant from morning till night, to the
strains of a large musical-box. Once a year only
does Torneå awaken from torpor into a state of
feverish activity, which commences on the 20th of
June and lasts for about a month—for at this
season the town is crowded with tourists who
come from all parts to see the sun shine at midnight. Every hotel and all available lodgings
are then crowded with guests, and the Haparanda
innkeepers also reap a fine harvest. The best
place from which to witness the phenomenon is
Mount Avasaksa, 800 feet high, about fifty miles
north of Torneå. Here the sun is visible at midnight for about a fortnight, but only appears
actually above the horizon for three days. At
this time of the year Torneå swarms with
mosquitos, for where these pests are concerned
Lapland almost out-rivals Alaska. For those
who decide to brave them, however, it may be
well to show how Avasaksa is best reached
from Torneå. A "karra" can be procured
from the Staåts Hotel, or, indeed, any other,
but Mr. Anderson, the landlord of the aforesaid

hostelry, understands the job better than anyone
else.

The post-stations are :—

Kakkola	.	.	9 English miles.
Korpikyla	.	.	9 ,, ,,
Pekkila	.	.	11 ,, ,,
Niemis	.	.	9 ,, ,,
Matarengi	.	.	8 ,, ,,

Bread, eggs, and milk can be had at all these
stations, but the accommodation is rough.

Matarengi is in Swedish territory, and from
here you may walk (or go by boat) to the
foot of the mountain, under three miles distant.
But if you visit Avasakṣa (in summer) do not
forget to take a plentiful supply of mosquito
netting, oil of cloves, and last, but not least,
patience.

Towards the end of July Torneå relapses into
her normal state of stagnation. There is absolutely nothing to do or talk about but the rare items
of stale news issued by the one primitive weekly
newspaper. When I arrived the Duke of the
Abruzzi had just accomplished his famous polar
voyage, and this was absolutely the sole topic
of conversation during my stay of three days!
In winter-time Torneå only enjoys three hours
of daylight in the twenty-four hours, but it is then

visited by a large number of Laplanders, who arrive from the Far North with sleigh-loads of reindeer tongues, hams, and skins for sale or barter. This is also a cause of temporary activity. But, summer or winter, the frontier town is a wretched place. Oddly enough, the Russian Church is its only picturesque edifice—a really beautiful little building, but there are only about a dozen Russians here to attend it!

The "spy mania" is rife in Torneå. I had not been there two hours before I was warned to be careful, although you may travel from end to end of Russia proper and speak your mind, as an Englishman, without fear of the consequences. But Torneå appeared to hold a monopoly as regards spies — although why secret agents should be stationed in this dead-alive settlement was a mystery. A quantity of proscribed literature finds its way here, by hand, across the river from Haparanda, which could hardly be the case if strict surveillance really existed. I heard a deal about spies in nearly every Finnish town I visited, but I fancy the rumours were much exaggerated, for, indeed, the services of secret agents in law-abiding, peaceable Finland would obviously be superfluous. It seems more probable that the Torneå system of espion-

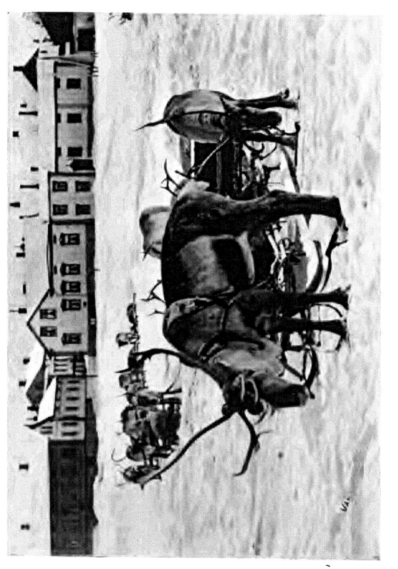

A WINTER SCENE

To face page 276

age (if it really existed) was designed to guard against Swedish intrigue—for the hatred of all the Swedes I met for the Russians far exceeded that of the Finns. The following incident bears this out.

"How far do you call it from the Russian side of the river?" I asked a Swede, whom I casually met on a ramble through Haparanda. "*Finland* is about half a mile from us," was the quiet reply, with an accent on the first word; "I know nothing about Russia"!

The aspect of Haparanda is perhaps less depressing, on the whole, than Torneå. Its houses are chiefly of wood, although a large and imposing stone structure—a new hotel—is being erected in their midst to meet the requirements of the new railway. And this is the only sign of advanced civilisation, for the streets are desolate, while the best shops resemble those of the "general" order in English country villages, where you may buy anything from eggs and butter to a suit of clothes. Towards the close of summer both towns are generally swept by strong gales, and outdoor exercise is rendered a questionable pleasure by clouds of dust. I missed little, therefore, by being confined to my room during the greater part of my stay by a sharp attack of gastritis, brought on by tinned and tainted salmon. My medicine chest had been presented to a friend in Vasa, and the Torneå practitioner did not inspire me with confidence; but luckily I still possessed the remains of a bottle of "Lactopeptine,"* an invaluable remedy in stomach disorders. In this case it acted like a charm, and I was able to resume my journey without the delay that would undoubtedly have arisen but for these magic tablets, which had already proved invaluable to me in north-eastern Siberia during an attempted land journey from New York to Paris.

The inhabitants of Torneå and Haparanda differ little in appearance, but the Finns compare favourably in one respect with their Swedish neighbours. I crossed Finland without once encountering an inebriate of either sex, while one day in Haparanda I met a dozen drunken men in the course of a short walk. A couple of these worthies, of whom I inquired my way, insisted on accompanying me to the Post Office and thence to my hotel, where I could not prevent them from following me into my private apartment. By this time I discovered that both men were very drunk—a fact previously over-

* Made by John M. Richards, 46, Holborn Viaduct, E.C.

TORNEÂ—HAPARANDA
(Russo-Swedish Frontier)

To face page 278

looked; and it was only by providing my un-
invited guests with additional refreshment that
they finally left me in peace! Both were Swedes.
One had been in South Africa, and spoke English
fluently, but the other's vocabulary was limited to
"Scotch-good." He was probably alluding to the
whisky, not to the people! His friend was less
complimentary, for everything British, even the
language, appeared to excite his displeasure.
"Do you know how English was invented?" he
asked, as my host quietly, but forcibly, expelled
him from the room. "Why, they boiled up all
the languages in a cauldron, and yours came to
the top, and was skimmed off like fat. No one
took the trouble to throw it away, and so it
remains!" which, however, the speaker did not,
for a false step (and perhaps some slight assistance from the landlord) suddenly projected him
from the top to the bottom of a conveniently
steep flight of stairs!

The steamers trading with Luleå and other
ports lie at Samli, a port about eight miles from
Torneå. A gale was raging on the night of my
departure, and the cart in which I drove to the
ship was once nearly upset by its force. I therefore expected a dirty night at sea, but when
we sailed at midnight the motion was hardly

perceptible, although the wind howled through the rigging with unabated fury. I had forgotten that a greater part of this route lies through almost land-locked fjords, formed by innumerable and well-wooded islands.

The journey to Luleå occupies about twelve hours, and I would willingly have prolonged it, for the *Norra-sverige*,* a roomy craft of 600 tons, was less like a merchant vessel than a yacht, with luxurious cabins, electric light, and even pianos to beguile the voyage. But Swedish passenger boats are generally comfortable, and always clean, and I am not sure that neatly clad, obliging stewardesses are not an improvement on the unkempt and often surly steward. I was afforded practical demonstration that navigation in this part of the Gulf is intricate, and sometimes risky, for, nearing Luleå, the steamer grounded with a crash that, to the inexperienced, sounded ominous. But the captain went on with his breakfast, and no one seemed in the least surprised, so I resumed the seat at table which I had vacated with less dignity than haste. For it appeared that these little incidents were of daily occurrence. "No rocks," said the

---

* These ships run direct to Stockholm from Torneå, touching at intermediate ports.

skipper, calmly sipping his coffee, "only sand"; and he added that Luleå is approached by a narrow channel, on either side of which there is often only a couple of feet of water. Wrecks, therefore, frequently occur, but are seldom attended by loss of life, for land is generally within easy distance, and, thanks to the protection of reefs and islands, a really heavy sea is unknown here.

The time at my disposal would not admit of a visit to Yelivara, an eight hours' journey by rail from Luleå, where there is an iron mine of prodigious richness. From another point of view Yelivara is also an interesting place, for it is reached by the most northern railway in the world, the terminus of which is fifty miles within the Arctic Circle. Even the Klondike line does not approach this parallel! A mining engineer on board the *Norra-sverige* told me that this part of Sweden teems with mineral wealth of all kinds (chiefly iron) and that there are plenty of openings for the capitalist, especially as the Swedish Government encourages foreign enterprise. He also informed me that parts of Russian Lapland would well repay the gold prospector, and, as regards this, his prophecy was a correct one, for important discoveries of the precious

metal have since been made on the Ivalojoki
River, about two hundred miles north of Torneå.
The fortunate finder hails, I believe, from Dawson
City.

I only remained one day at Luleå, but it was a
very pleasant one, and being a Sunday, the town
wore a holiday aspect, the gaiety of which was
enhanced by a blue sky and brilliant sunshine.
Church bells were chiming merrily, flags waved,
and a military band sounded from somewhere
in the distance as I landed and made my way
through the crowded streets to the Restaurant
Wibell, the best, by the way, in the place.
Here an excellent *déjeuner* was served while
an orchestra of wandering gipsies recalled the
delights of " Armenonville " and " Madrid " in far-
away Lutetia. But a rude shock awaited me,
for, at the end of the meal, Finnish marks were
refused in payment. Nor were my digestion
or temper improved by driving about the town
for an hour in search of a money-changer, who
finally turned up by chance in the person of a
Frankfort Jew, travelling in fancy goods. This
gentleman was kind enough to oblige me with
change (at the moderate charge of about fifty
per cent.), and I left Luleå at the appointed
hour, 4 p.m., with a conviction that Northern

Sweden, in some respects, needs reform. At any rate, it is better to obviate these annoyances by converting Finnish money into Swedish at Torneå or Haparanda. There is a bank in the latter place where you are sure of a current rate of exchange, which, it is needless to add, I did not obtain from my Hebrew friend at Luleå.

From Luleå to Stockholm by land is a long and tiresome journey, and the best plan for those who can afford the time is to travel by sea. Considering the distance the railway fare is very moderate (thirty-four kroners), but I would gladly have paid three times the amount to have travelled at, say, thirty miles an hour—north of the capital twenty-five is apparently looked upon as a breakneck rate of speed! The best carriages are not called first, but second class, as in Finland, and are on the corridor system, but in these remote districts the " waggon-restaurant " does not exist. Nor are sleeping-cars provided, for at eleven o'clock on the first evening we were told to alight at a lonely station in the woods, as the journey would not be resumed until six o'clock on the following morning. By the time the guard had thoroughly explained the situation, every bed and sofa in the miserable station hotel had been appropriated by our numerous passengers. Snow lay on the ground, and a sharp frost was not conducive to an open-air *siesta*, while, although it remained all night alongside the platform, permission to sleep in the train was refused. Fortunately the stationmaster knew of a place about a mile away where shelter was obtainable, and I tramped off, accompanied by a lad with a lantern, through the forest to the hut of a wood-cutter. Here I managed to find a shake-down and a doze until 5 a.m., when it was time to return to the train. I could not ascertain why travellers should be subjected to all this discomfort. Only one so-called express leaves Luleå daily for Stockholm, and there is always this tedious wait and scramble for sleeping accommodation at Jörn. It is well to telegraph to the latter from Luleå for a bed, but even then it is not always easy to secure one.

A second day in the train drew wearily to a close. The picturesque scenery passed through would have been enjoyable enough under ordinary circumstances, but our crawling rate of progression would have irritated Job himself. The snail-like speed was partly explained by a brass plate on the engine, which bore the name of a well-known English firm, but the date of its manufacture

was 1863, and this for a mail train! Decent
meals *en route* would perhaps have lightened the
burden of those weary hours, but the restaurants
were not alluring, and infinitely inferior to those
on the Finnish lines. Happily, on the second
night, beds were made up in the carriages,
and the following morning we reached Stockholm after a journey of over thirty hours, which
might easily have been accomplished in half the
time.

And here, alighting at the Grand Hotel, I bid
the reader farewell, for we are once more on a
well-beaten track of tourist travel. Seated the
same evening after dinner, over coffee and a
cigarette, in the glittering hall of a palatial hotel,
the sad and stirring strains of Hungary carry me
back in memory to that wild and beautiful land of
Suomi, now, alas! a vision of the past. And the
journey from beginning to end is recalled as a
brief but pleasant dream—the stately parks and
palaces of Helsingfors, glorious Imatrá, and quaint
old Nyslott; Tammerfors, with its busy streets
and factories, and my hearty welcome at primitive
but hospitable "Oulu." Distance lends enchant-
ment even to my recollections of Torneå, which
renewed acquaintance with that dreary town
would no doubt speedily efface. But no matter;

a few weeks have been wasted, perhaps, but at any rate, more than delightfully wasted, in that great little country of picturesque patriotism, Finland, a country which I earnestly pray that a kindly fate may some day permit me to revisit.

CHAPTER XVIII

HOW TO GET TO FINLAND

IN conclusion, I may as well give a few hints for the guidance of those who may be induced, by this very inadequate description of its charms, to visit one of the quaintest and most delightful countries in Europe. Being aware of the difficulty of obtaining particulars in London as to communications, etc., in Finland, I made it my business during my stay there to obtain information regarding time-tables, distances, fares, etc., from the steamship lines and local railway officials, which it would be next to impossible to procure in England. Readers not interested in the subject can now close this volume, but others may care to know how Finland is to be reached as comfortably, quickly, and cheaply as possible, either by the impecunious sportsman or the tourist wearied of commonplace travelling experiences.

Roughly speaking, there are three routes, viz.

(1) overland *viâ* Calais, Germany, and Russia ; (2) *viâ* Calais, Copenhagen, and Stockholm; and (3) by sea direct from Hull.

Indifferent sailors and those for whom the sea has no charms may reach Finland without undergoing a longer period of discomfort than that entailed by the short passage across the Straits of Dover. This is, of course, the quickest and most luxurious route. You enter at Calais a "train de luxe," with waggon-lits and restaurant cars, and reach your destination within a few hours, that is if you travel by the "Nord Express." At the same time, a single first-class fare from London to Helsingfors by this route amounts to nearly £20, exclusive of meals and expenses *en route*, and my object is to show how Finland may be visited for, say, three weeks, at a total expenditure of, perhaps, £5 more than that sum.

Route No. 2, *viâ* Copenhagen and Stockholm, is better suited to those of moderate means. It necessitates, however, several hours of sea, viz. from Dover to Calais, Copenhagen to Malmö, and Stockholm to Åbo or Helsingfors. The second passage takes about an hour, the third is a steamer run of twenty hours, but in summer-time the Baltic is generally smooth and pleasant, and most of the course is laid through straits and fjords formed by thousands of islands and well protected from the wind and waves. Indeed, there are only two hours of really open sea between Stockholm by way of Queenborough, Flushing, and the Hook of Holland, but as, even during the summer months, a nasty roll is often encountered in the North Sea, and as these passages are much longer (and not much cheaper) than *via* Dover and Calais, I do not recommend them to the sea-sick traveller. The following are the approximate fares, overland, from London to Helsingfors :—

ROUTE I.

Via Calais, Berlin, and St. Petersburg: Fare, exclusive of sleeping-car (first class), £16 18s. 10d. (60 hours).

ROUTE II.

Via Calais, Copenhagen, and Stockholm (first class), £13 1s. 9d. (70 hours).
Via Flushing (first class), £9 5s. 9d. (71 hours).
Via Hook of Holland (first class), £9 3s. 9d.(74 hours).

Finally there is route No. 3—by sea direct from Hull, and this is certainly the best (and cheapest) one for those who are not victims of *mal-de-mer*. The Finland Steamship Company, which is undoubtedly the line to travel by,

2 P.

keeps up an all-the-year-round service by the *Arcturus* and *Polaris*, new and powerful fifteen-knot steamers fitted throughout with electric light and with accommodation for seventy saloon, and thirty second-class, passengers. These sister-ships resemble miniature ocean-liners, with their broad promenade decks, palatial saloons, and large, airy state-rooms, all amidships. A ladies' boudoir and comfortable smoking-room are also provided, so that the most modern requirements of luxurious sea-travel are fulfilled, while to ensure safety the vessels are divided into water-tight compartments. There is a first-class cuisine on board, and Finnish customs are observed. Coffee or tea with biscuits from 7 to 9 a.m., lunch from 9 till 10 a.m., consisting of the national "smör-gasbord" and followed by a dainty and well-cooked "*déjeuner.*" Dinner, the principal meal of the day, is served at 3.30, and at about 9 p.m. supper ends the day. Wines, beer, and mineral waters are extra. This daily meal is not, as usual, included in the fare, but charged for at the rate of 6*s.* and 4*s.* per diem, first and second class. A first-class single ticket from Hull to Helsingfors costs £5, and £8 return (second class: £3 single, £5 return), and a journey made under such comfortable conditions is well worth the money. To this must be added the return fares between London and Hull, and you have your travelling expenses, outside Finland itself, to a fraction. Bicycles are charged a freight of 6s. each. The *Arcturus* and *Polaris* sail according to tide, but not before 4 p.m., every Saturday from Hull to Helsingfors, touching at Copenhagen. Another of their boats, the *Astrea*, sails every alternate Wednesday for Åbo, also calling at Copenhagen. It may be added that the attendance on board these vessels is excellent, and that most of the officials speak English.

In fine weather (which prevails during summer) the passage, lasting about three and a half days, is most enjoyable, for the brilliant sunshine and blue skies of the Baltic recall those of the Mediterranean, although the pure sea-breezes are untainted by that curse of the Ligurian coasts, the "mistral." Leaving the North Sea, we pass the Skageräck, Kattegat, and Sound, with glorious views on either side, and on a clear day catch sight of Elsinore, with its ruined castle, the resting-place of Hamlet the Dane. On the Monday afternoon Copenhagen is reached, and as the steamer does not leave again until the morning of the following day, there is time for a stroll through the quaint old city with its primitive buildings, shady squares, and clean, broad streets. Then away again, to skirt the Swedish coast for a time, as our vessel cleaves the cold, dark waves of the Baltic until the quaint old island of Gotland with its numerous towers rises above the horizon. Shortly after this we enter a dense archipelago of islands, to emerge from it, almost sorry that the voyage is at an end, at our destination, Helsingfors.

Finland now lies before us. Where shall we go? All depends upon what we have come for, sport or travel. If the former, Imatrá or Kajana must be made for, and the first-named is the nearest. Kajana * should not be attempted unless we have a good three weeks to spare, in which case we can also try Vaala, where salmon (fifty pounds) are caught, and the grayling run from three to five and a half pounds; or Ontojoki, where, for once in a way, we need not hire a boat to fish from. If time is of no object we might even penetrate as far as Tsirka-Kemi, the best place for grayling in the world, where an Englishman once landed two hundred during one summer afternoon. But Tsirka-Kemi is in the Russian

* Permission to fish in the lakes and streams around Kajana can be procured in that town from Herr Herman Renfors, whose hospitality is proverbial, and who is always willing to furnish information regarding sport.

Karelen, one hundred and thirty miles east of Kajana, and to reach it means time and money, and we have not come to Finland to waste either. Near Kajana there is plenty of good rough shooting during the season from August to December. Capercailzie, wild duck, black-cock and hazel grouse abound; also, occasionally, ptarmigan. But there are hundreds of good places, both for fishing and shooting, which can only be heard of on arrival in the country. In any case, the sportsman must be guided, to a great extent, by the season and local conditions, and a visit to Lindebäck's Sporting Magazine, in Helsingfors, will soon put him on the right track, whether the month be May or September, or his destination be Tsirka-Kemi or Imatrá.

If we have come to Finland only to find rest and relaxation, to dawdle away the summer days in lazy enjoyment of pure air and glorious scenery, it is best to remain in the capital for a few days and then to decide upon one of the following routes, which have been planned especially for those who have not too much time at their disposal.

2 Q

Tour No. 1.

This will occupy about Fifteen Days.

Helsingfors—Viborg	. .	Steamer
Viborg—Rattijarvi .	. .	Steamer
Rattijarvi—Imatrá .	. .	Mail Coach
Imatrá—Jakosenranta	.	Mail Coach
Jakosenranta—Villmanstrand	.	L. Steamer*
Villmanstrand—Nyslott (Punkaharju) .	. .	L. Steamer
Nyslott—Kuopio .	. .	L. Steamer
Kuopio—Idensalmi.	. .	L. Steamer
Idensalmi—Kajana .	. .	Mail Coach
Kajana—Vaala .	. .	L. Steamer
Vaala—Muhos .	. .	Rowing-boat
Muhos—Uleåborg .	. .	L. Steamer
Uleåborg—Vasa .	. .	Railway
Vasa—Helsingfors .	. .	Railway or Steamer

Total cost, £21.

Tour No. 2.

About Nine Days.

Helsingfors or Åbo—Viborg	.	Steamer
Viborg—Rattijarvi .	. .	Steamer
Imatrá—Jakosenranta	.	Mail Coach
Jakosenranta—Villmanstrand	.	L. Steamer
Villmanstrand—Nyslott	.	L. Steamer

(From Nyslott visit Punkaharju by L. Steamer.)

Nyslott—Kuopio .	.	L. Steamer
Kuopio — Helsingfors, Åbo, or Hangö .	. .	Railway

Total cost, £17.

* Lake steamer.

TOUR No. 3.

About Six Days.

Helsingfors or Åbo—Viborg	.	Steamer or Railway
Viborg—Imatrá . .	.	Railway
Imatrá—Jakosenranta	.	Mail Coach
Jakosenranta—Villmanstrand	.	L. Steamer
Villmanstrand—Nyslott	.	L. Steamer

(From Nyslott visit Punkaharju by L. Steamer.)

Nyslott—Villmanstrand	.	L. Steamer
Villmanstrand—Helsingfors, Åbo, or Hangö .	.	Railway

Total cost, £15 10s.

TOUR No. 4.

About Five Days.

Helsingfors or Åbo—Viborg	.	Steamer
Viborg—Joensuu . .	.	L. Steamer

(Visit Punkaharju on the way.)

Joensuu—Sordavala.	.	Railway
Sordavala—Imatrá .	.	Railway
Imatrá—Helsingfors or Åbo	.	Railway

Total cost, £15.

TOUR No. 5.

About Four Days.

Helsingfors or Åbo—Viborg	.	Steamer
Viborg—Rattijarvi .	.	L. Steamer
Rattijarvi—Imatrá .	.	Mail Coach
Imatrá—Helsingfors	.	.

Total cost, £14.

The above sums represent the approximate total cost of each journey, including first-class return fare to Hull, meals during the sea passage, and expenses in Finland, which are estimated at 8*s.* per diem—a fair allowance. Tickets for all of these tours are issued by the Finland Steamship Company, and the railway and lake journeys are easily combined with the weekly sailings of their steamers from Hull. A second-class passage on the *Arcturus* or *Polaris* reduces the cost of each trip by about £4.

The best months in Finland are August and September. June is also delightful, but for many reasons probably not so convenient for English travellers. Chilly or delicate persons should leave the country before October, for winter comes on with sudden severity. A fur coat and plenty of rugs should therefore be taken by those going as far north as Torneå. Light and heavy homespun and serge suits are the best, and woollen underclothing should always be worn, notwithstanding the often excessive heat at midday, for at sundown the fall of temperature is generally considerable. Mosquitos are troublesome. Take, therefore, a couple of small sleeping-nets, two or three gauze veils (to entirely cover the head), and stout dogskin gloves, with a cloth or canvas flap sewn on to button round the sleeve to protect the wrist, a very vulnerable point. As an additional precaution, a bottle of essential oil of cloves should be included in the medicine chest, which latter is essential in the remoter districts. A small tabloid medicine case, containing also some simple surgical appliances, was specially fitted up for this journey under my direction by Messrs. Burroughs, Wellcome, and Co., of Snow Hill Buildings, London, E.C. The tabloids retain their qualities in all climates, and are a great boon where space is limited. A case exactly similar to mine may be obtained from the makers at a trifling cost.

If you are a fisherman, it is well to take a few cheap presents for guides and boatmen, for most of your fishing must be done afloat, and little attentions are always gratefully received by the peasantry. Good strong clasp-knives and English briar-root pipes are especially prized. Do not take a great amount of English tobacco for your own smoking, for it can be procured at Helsingfors, where it will cost you less than to bring it into the country through the Custom-house.

The safest and most convenient way of carrying money is in circular notes, which can be cashed at most of the principal towns. You can easily ascertain the current rate of exchange in any newspaper. The only lawful currency for payment above ten marks are pieces of ten and twenty marks in gold, but Bank of Finland notes are more used than gold, and, being at par, are equally convenient.

Tickets from Hull to Finland may be obtained in London from Messrs. Good and Redmayne, 14, Lombard Street, who, as agents for the Finland Steamship Company, will furnish all requisite information regarding the country and its communications. Mr. Lars Krogius, the Company's agent, of 9, West Quay, Helsingfors, is also British Vice-Consul, and is ever ready to advise and assist English travellers.

Finally, let me earnestly advise those in quest of health, pleasure, or sport at a moderate cost to forsake, for once in a way, their favourite Swiss mountain or Italian lake in favour of Finland for a summer holiday. They will not regret it.

THE END

APPENDIX A

SOME FINNISH WORDS LIKELY TO BE USEFUL TO SPORTSMEN

Above	.	*Paalla*	Black-cock .	*Teiri*
After .	.	*Takana*	Blanket .	*Villa peite*
Afternoon .		*Ehtoo-puoli*	Boat . .	*Vene*
Again .	.	*Taas*	Boatman .	*Soutaja*
All .	.	*Kaiki*	Brandy .	*Viina*
Also .	.	*Myos*	Bread . .	*Vehna leipaa*
Always	.	*Aina*	Breakfast .	*Murkina*
And .	.	*Ya*	Bream .	*Lahna*
Another	.	*Toinen*	Broken .	*Rikottu*
Arrive .	.	*Tulla*	Bugs . .	*Luteita*
Ashore	.	*Maalle*	Butter .	*Voita*
Autumn	.	*Siksi*	Buy . .	*Ostar*
Bad .	.	*Paha*	Call . .	*Kutsua*
Bait .	.	*Syotti*	Candle. .	*Kintila*
Basket .	.	*Kori*	Capercailzie.	*Metso*
Bathe (to)	.	*Kylpeä*	Cart . .	*Kärrit*
Bear .	.	*Karhu*	Cartridge .	*Patruni*
Bed .	.	*Sänky*	Catch (to) .	*Saada*
Beer .	.	*Olutta*	Cheap .	*Halpa*
Best .	.	*Paras*	Cheese .	*Justoa*
Big .	.	*Suuri*	Chicken .	*Kananpoika*
Little	.	*Pieni*	Chub . .	*Särki*

299

Church	.	*Kirkko*	Fish-line .	*Ongen-sima*
Claret .		*Bordeaux Vini*	Fishing-rod .	*Ongen-vapa*
Coffee .	.	*Kavia*	Float . .	*Lautta*
Cold .	.	*Kylma*	Fly . .	*Kärpänen*
Cord .	.	*Nuora*	Fog . .	*Sumu*
Corkscrew	.	*Korkiruvi*	Ford . .	*Kalamo*
Cut (to)	.	*Leikata*	Forget. .	*Unhotaa*
Danger	.	*Vaara*	Forwards .	*Eteen-pain*
Day .	.	*Paiva*	Fox . .	*Repo*
Dear .	.	*Kallis*	Freeze (to) .	*Jaatya*
Deer .	.	*Peura*	Fur coat .	*Turki*
Directly	.	*Suoran-straxt*	Further .	*Edempana*
Doctor	.	*Tohtori*	Gaff . .	*Koukku*
Dog .	.	*Koira*	Game	
Drink (to)	.	*Juoda*	(feathered)	*Metsa-rista*
Early .	.	*Varhain*	Gently. .	*Hilja*
Late	.	*Myohan*	Get (to) .	*Ulottua*
East .	.	*Ita*	Give (to) .	*Antar*
Eat (to)	.	*Syoda*	Grayling .	*Harjus*
Eggs .	.	*Munia*	Grouse .	*Pyy*
Englishman .		*Englantilai-*	Gun . .	*Pyssy*
		nen	Gunpowder .	*Rutia*
Enough	.	*Kylla*	Hare . .	*Janis*
Evening	.	*Ilta*	Help . .	*Apu*
Everywhere .		*Kaikialla*	Hold (to) .	*Pitaa*
Falls .	.	*Koski*	Hotel . .	*Hotelli*
Fast .	.	*Kiristi*	Hungry .	*Nalkainen*
Firewood	.	*Puita*	I .	*Mina*
Fish .	.	*Kala*	You . .	*Te*
Fish (to)	.	*Onkia*	Ice . .	*Yar*
Fisherman	.	*Kalastaja*	Ill . .	*Sairas*
Fish-hook	.	*Ongen-koukku*	Important .	*Tarkea*

Ink	*Lakki*		No	*Ei*
Interpreter	*Tulkki*		Yes	*Ya-ninn*
Island	*Saari*		Noon	*Puolen paivan aika*
Keep (to)	*Pitaa*		North	*Pohja*
Knife	*Veitsi*		Nothing	*Ei mittan*
Lake	*Yarvi*		Now	*Nyt*
Later	*Myohaisempi*		Oar	*Airo*
Laundress	*Pesuakka*		Often	*Usein*
Let go	*Pastakka*		Omelet	*Omeletti*
Lose (to)	*Kadotta*		Opposite	*Vastoin-pain*
Luggage	*Kapinit*		Partridge	*Metsakana*
Man	*Iminen*		Pay (to)	*Maksa*
Map	*Karta*		Pen	*Pänna*
Matches	*Tuli-tikkuja*		Pencil	*Lijispanna*
Me	*Minulle*		Paper	*Paperia*
You	*Te*		Perch	*Ahven*
Milk	*Maitoa*		Pike (fish)	*Hauki*
Money	*Raha*		Pin	*Nuppa-Neula*
Minnows			Pipe	*Pippu*
(artificial)	*Uistin*		Pocket-book	*Musito-kirja*
Much	*Paljo*		Police	*Polissi*
Little	*Vahan*		Post Office	*Posti-Kontori*
More	*Viela*		Post-station	*Keskievari*
Near	*Liki*		Post-horses	*Kitihevosia*
Far	*Kaukana*		Provisions	*Muona*
Needle	*Neula*		Ptarmigan	*Riekko*
Net	*Verko*		Railway Station	
Net (landing)	*Havas*			*Rautatien Asema*
Never	*Ei Koskan*		Rain	*Sade*
Night	*Yo*		Ready	*Valmis*
Morning	*Amu*		Reel (fishing)	*Rulla*
Night (at)	*Yolla*		Reindeer	*Peura*

Return (to)		*Palata Takaisin*	Sometimes	. *Joskus*
Reward	.	*Palkita*	South .	. *Etela*
River .	.	*Yoki*	Spring (the) .	*Kevat*
Roach	.	*Sorva*	Start (to)	. *Lahtea*
Road .	.	*Tie*	Steamer	. *Hoyrylaiva*
Robber	.	*Rosvo*	Storm	. *Myrsky*
Rope .	.	*Koysi*	String	. *Nyori*
Row (to)	.	*Soota*	Sugar .	. *Sokeria*
Russia	.	*Venäjänmaa*	Summer	. *Kesa*
Sable .	.	*Sapeli*	Take (to)	. *Ottar*
Salmon	.	*Loki*	Tea .	. *Teeta*
Salt .	.	*Suola*	Thread	. *Rima*
Scissors	.	*Sakset*	Tired	. *Vasinit*
Sea .	.	*Meri*	Tobacco	. *Tupakka*
See (to)	.	*Nada*	To-day	*Tana paivana*
Send (to)	.	*Lahetta*	To-morrow .	*Huomenna*
Shallow	.	*Matala*	To-night	. *Tana Yona*
Deep		*Syva*	Too much .	*Lika Paljo*
Shoot (to) .		*Ampua*	Towel	. *Kasilina*
Shot (lead)		*Haulia*	Trout .	. *Forelli*
Show (to) .		*Nayttaa*	Village	. *Kyla*
Side (on this)		*Talla puolella*	Waiter	. *Passari*
Side (on the other)		*Toisella puolella*	Walk (to) .	*Kavella*
			Water	. *Vetta*
Silence	.	*Hiljaisus*	West .	. *Lansi*
Silk thread		*Silki*	Wet .	. *Marka*
Sleep (to) .		*Maata*	When ?	. *Koska*
Slowly	.	*Hitasti*	Where ?	. *Missa*
Snipe	.	*Kurpa*	Which	. *Mika*
Snow	.	*Lumi*	Why .	. *Miksi*
Soap	.	*Saipua*	Why not ? .	*Miksei*
			Who .	. *Kuka*

Wide	.	*Avara*	Wolf . .	*Susi*
Wind	.	*Tuli*	Year . .	*Vuosi*
Wine	.	*Vini*	Yesterday .	*Eilen*
Winter	.	*Talvi*	Your . .	*Teidan*
Woman	.	*Nais-Iminen*		

MONTHS

April	.	*Huhtiku*	August .	*Eloku*
May	.	*Toukoku*	September .	*Sysku*
June	.	*Kesaku*	October .	*Lokaku*
July	.	*Heinaku*		

DAYS OF THE WEEK

Monday	.	*Manantai*	Friday. .	*Perjantai*
Tuesday	.	*Tistai*	Saturday .	*Lauantai*
Wednesday	.	*Keskivikka*	Sunday .	*Sunnuntai*
Thursday	.	*Torstai*		

NUMERALS

1	*Iksi*	7	*Seitseman*
2	*Kaksi*	8	*Kadeksan*
3	*Kolme*	9	*Ideksan*
4	*Nelja*	10	*Kymennen*
5	*Visi*	11	*Iksi Toista*
6	*Kusi*	12	*Kaksi Toista*

Add *Toista* to each number up to

20 *Kaksi-Kymenta*
21 *Kaksimenta-Iksi*
22 *Kaksimenta-Kaksi*

Add the unit up to ten and then

30	*Kolmekymenta*	80	*Kadeksan-Kymenta*
40	*Nelja Kymenta*	90	*Ideksan-Kymenta*
50	*Visi Kymenta*	100	*Sata*
60	*Kusi Kymenta*	500	*Visi-Sata*
70	*Seitseman Kymenta*	1000	*Tuhat*

APPENDIX B

LIST OF THE BEST HOTELS, PHYSICIANS, CHEMISTS, ETC., IN THE PRINCIPAL TOWNS OF FINLAND

ÅBO.

Hotel	. .	" Societetshuset "
Doctor	. .	G. Hahl
Chemist	. .	Emil Reims
Bookseller	. .	Herman Edgren
Rod and Gunmaker		J. Osterblad

BJORNEBORG.

Hotel	. .	" Otava "
Doctor	. .	F. Ligeblad
Chemist	. .	J. Juselius
Bookseller	. .	Satakunta Bokhandeln
Rod and Gunmaker		Nya Järhandeln

GAMLA-KARLEBY.

Hotel	. .	" Societetshuset "
Doctor	. .	A. Strengell
Chemist	. .	F. Lofjelm
Bookseller . .	}	J. Bjorkmann
Rod and Gunmaker		

2 R

ULEÅBORG.

Hotel	. .	" Societetshuset "
Doctor	. .	Granberg
Chemist	. .	Gamla Aptaket
Bookseller	. .	O. Jalander*
Rod and Gunmaker		L. Fabritius

VASA—NIKOLAISTAD.

Hotel	. .	" Central "
Doctor	. .	K. Ekholm
Chemist	. .	J. Lindeback
Bookseller	. .	K. Montin *
Rod and Gunmaker		Danielson and Kurten

French books, volumes of the Tauchnitz edition, and good maps of the country may be procured from booksellers marked with an asterisk.

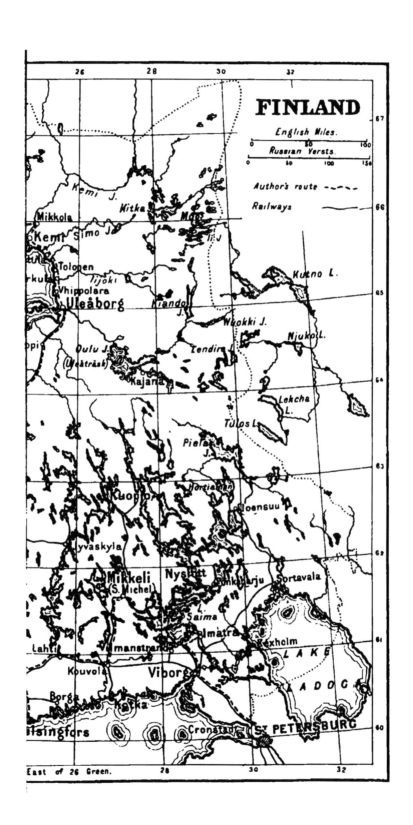

HANGÖ.

Hotel	. .	"Grand"
Doctor	. .	E. Chydenius
Chemist	. .	H. Lindgren
Bookseller	. .	A. Kanstell
Rod and Gunmaker		J. Nillson

HELSINGFORS.

Hotel	. .	"Societetshuset"
"	. .	"Kamp"
"	. .	"Fennia"

(Porters meet trains and steamers)

Chemist	. .	Stiggelius Apotek
Bookseller	. .	G. Edlund *
Rod and Gunmaker		Lindeback's Sport Magazine

JAKOBSTAD.

Hotel	. .	"Societetshuset"
Doctor	. .	H. Backman
Chemist	. .	K. Candolin
Bookseller	. . }	F. Petersen
Rod and Gunmaker	}	

KAJANA.

Hotel	. .	Turist-Hotellet
Doctor	. .	O. Wennerstrom
Chemist	. .	P. Stenius
Bookseller	. .	Jenny Bergh
Rod and Gunmaker		H. Renfors

KUOPIO.

Hotel	. .	" Societetshuset "
Doctor	. .	A. Puspanen
Chemist	. .	J. Johnsson
Bookseller	. .	S. Kastegrens*
Rod and Gunmaker		J. Carlson

NYSTAD.

Hotel	. .	"Valhalla "
Doctor	. .	K. Rostedt
Chemist	. .	J. Malmlund
Bookseller	. .	H. Winter
Rod and Gunmaker		A. Klingstedt

TAMMERFORS.

Hotel	. .	" Societetshuset "
Doctor	. .	Idman
Chemist	. .	Borg
Bookseller	. .	Lytikainen*
Rod and Gunmaker		V. Sandberg

TAVASTEHUS.

Hotel	. .	" Societetshuset "
Doctor	. .	A. W. Manner
Chemist	. .	F. Schamman
Bookseller	. .	Rytkonen *
Rod and Gunmaker		E. Wallennius

BILLING AND SONS, LTD., PRINTERS, GUILDFORD